C000156192

Praise for *Confessions of a Middle-Aged Hippie*

"In *Confessions of a Middle-Aged Hippie,* author Beverley Golden brings us back to the '60s with a fascinating and hilarious memoir that teaches us anything is possible when fueled by persistence, passion and conviction. Laced with poignant anecdotes and cameos of various celebrity personalities, the story pivots between the author's health issues and the entertainment industry with plenty of lessons learned from both.

A delightful storyteller and "Aquarian contrarian and paradigm shifter" with a great sense of humor, Golden offers readers a lively and poignant tale loaded with many cultural hot buttons: money, sex, food, relationships, motherhood, health, medicine, celebrities and entertainment – with a dash of metaphysics (astrology, past lives, karmic reunions) plus alternative medicine and healing. *Confessions of a Middle-Aged Hippie* has it all!

Most importantly, through Golden's story, readers learn to trust their intuition and never give up hope. Woven with practical and spiritual wisdom, this book offers an unusual tapestry of entertainment and enlightenment, perfect for today's Boomers and suitable for any generation seeking an uplifting read."

Catherine J. Rourke,
Editor & Publisher, The Sedona Observer/Conscious Media Evolution

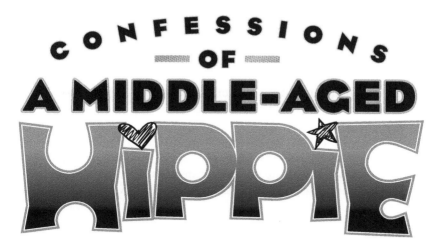

CONFESSIONS OF A MIDDLE-AGED HIPPIE

Observations of Life on Earth & Other Cosmic Meanderings

BEVERLEY GOLDEN

Cover and Interior Design by Joost DeVoot
Author Cover photographs by Denise Grant
Hippie Girl designed by Katherine Morley

www.beverleygolden.com

Library of Congress Cataloging-in-Publication Data

Golden, Beverley
Confessions of a Middle-Aged Hippie:
Observations of Life on Earth and Other Cosmic Meanderings

p. cm.
Paperback ISBN: 978-1-947708-81-5 • Ebook ISBN: 978-1-947708-83-9

Library of Congress Control Number: 2020918514

Second Edition, October 2020

CITRINE PUBLISHING
Schenectady, New York, U.S.A.
(828) 585-7030
www.CitrinePublishing.com

This book is a love letter to my family.

To my mother, Lillian, an indomitable spirit who always encouraged me to follow my dreams and allowed me to fly.

To my amazing daughter, Lani, whose light shines so brightly she shows me the way out of the darkness time after time.

To my brother, Niel, for his openness, calming support and musical inspiration.

To my ex, Doug, for being there to create so many of the adventures and memories I write about in this book.

And to my father, Louis, who I know is smiling down on me and continues to guide me, reminding me what unconditional love feels like. I only hope his gift of storytelling lives on in me.

Without the love of my family... none of my life stories would mean anything.

*And in the end, it's not the years in your life that count.
It's the life in your years.*

Abraham Lincoln *(The Original Hippie)*

Acknowledgments

Where to begin? "Begin at the beginning," the King said, very gravely, "and go on till you come to the end: then stop." – Lewis Carroll from *Alice in Wonderland*.

If only it were that easy. Although I rarely start anything at the beginning, if I did, the people I would want to thank would fill more pages than this entire book.

Of course, I want to thank everyone who has contributed to my bringing this book to the world: Tom Bird, Joost DeVoot, Catherine Rourke, Michael Smith, and my most incredible cheerleader and editor, Penelope Love.

To my amazing family, to whom this book is also dedicated: Lillian Golden, Louis Golden, Lani Billard, Niel Golden and Doug Billard. And my longtime friend Sharon Stern, for some unforgettable trips, memories that are still alive and her understanding friendship.

To those who have supported me in my lifelong healing journey. Most recently: Jane Kieran, Dr. Veronica Koopmans, Regine Kurek, Monica Palmer and Daniella Staub. And, to the late Dr. Ravi Devgan, for always being on the cutting edge of "new"– rest in peace and sorry I didn't get to say goodbye.

To all the skeptics who continually told me what was *not* possible based on statistics and science. Thanks for fueling me to show what really *is* possible in the realm of magic and miracles, when it comes to the human spirit.

Do I thank singer Daryl Hall and artist Peter Max for the incredible stories I share in this book?

To all those who remain unnamed in these pages, I hope you recognize yourself and thanks for the astonishing stories that came out of our interactions. To those who passed through and left your mark—teachers, gurus, doctors, healers, friends, family, business associates. You are all a part of this book.

"I can't go back to yesterday because I was a different person then." – Lewis Carroll from *Alice in Wonderland*. I encourage everyone to look at your own life, as a magnificent, ever-changing, always evolving, one-of-a-kind piece of art!

Preface to the Second Edition

It's hard to imagine the world of just seven years ago, 2013, when *Confessions of a Middle-Aged Hippie* was released. The world today is dramatically different and at times I find myself longing for those simpler times we often talk about when we reminisce about our childhood years.

This book is a love letter to my family, maybe even more so now than when I first published *Confessions*. As you read the pages and get to know all the people who contributed to my life and my stories, perhaps one of the most prominent is my beautiful mother, Lillian, and her indomitable spirit.

When I wrote the book, she was a lively 96 years old and still going strong, loving life and living it to the max. I say "was," as on January 25, 2020, she passed away at the incredible age of 103, just five weeks before her 104th birthday. As you read these pages, please imagine her alive and with us. May her shining spirit continue to inspire people who read about her, the way it did throughout her life.

It's been fascinating and heartwarming to hear what readers take away from *Confessions*. It makes me the happiest when readers resonate with my stories and feel open enough share their own stories with me. I believe our individual stories have the power to impact others in ways that we all grow, learn and heal. So, I invite you to reach out and connect with me, whether that be on social media or directly on my website via email. I look forward to hearing how *Confessions* has touched you!

Beverley Golden
October 2020

Contents

Acknowledgments | **vii**

Preface to the Second Edition | **xiii**

Prologue:
Revelation... You Can't Get a Good Book Down | **1**

In the Beginning | **6**

Who's Your Daddy? | **12**

You're Having Your Baby... Tomorrow | **25**

The '80s – Countdown to Number Three | **34**

Love and Blizzards... Maybe Mother Nature Really Does Know Best | **42**

Jammin' and Searching | **53**

Return From The Living Dead | **60**

You Too Can Write a Book in Eight Days | **89**

Take it to The Max | **96**

Seek and Sometimes Ye Shall Find | **104**

Past Lives, Reincarnation, Karmic Reunions and Daryl Hall | **113**

Food Glorious Food | **134**

A Bit About a Lot of Things – Money, Music, Family and More Food | **140**

Outrageous Encounters and an Excess of Exes | **156**

Filling in the Blanks | **183**

Wrapping it All Up... Not So Neatly | **201**

Prologue: Revelation...
You Can't Get a Good Book Down

Something magical happens when you sit down and finally tell your life story by committing it to the page. It's ironically a bit hard to put into words. It's thrilling and exhilarating. Mesmerizing. Cathartic. And even a bit scary. Sometimes all at the same time. Hopefully, with just enough insight to shine some light out into the world, too. But for me, that is not exactly how this book happened. Let me explain.

In preparing to go to the writing retreat I mention in Chapter 8, I began a daily ritual of walking while listening to a subliminal tape provided by the retreat facilitator, one that guided me back to my inner writer. Each of the participants had been instructed to absolutely NOT start writing anything down on paper. Yet somehow, the book began pouring out in a rather unusual way. As I walked and listened within, I was literally telling my life story to none other than *THE* Oprah Winfrey. At that time, even though her twenty-five-year network show was about to end, she appeared as I imagined her, always the eager listener in this inner conversation playing out in my head. She asked few questions and remained keen on letting me share my stories. In this fantastical reality, I was literally both characters. I'd tell my story and then proceed to ask the questions of myself! Having imaginary conversations in my head is something I'm in fact very familiar with.

At the time I was writing this book, every aspiring author shared the same desire: to have the unique, but rare opportunity to appear on *The Oprah Winfrey Show*. To be seated next to the queen of daytime talk television herself, and then to have an intimate conversation about your book broadcast to billions, would almost guarantee becoming a best-selling author, simply from one TV appearance. A wonderful possibility, but not an easy reality to accomplish. The writing itself may flow easily, but getting on *Oprah*? Not so easy.

So here I was, walking and silently having an ongoing conversation about my life, telling my stories in a most intimate way to my vision of how Oprah Winfrey was. This was all happening, very alive in fact, even if only in my head. It would be unlikely I could write a book and use Oprah as a character in it, without cutting through lots of red tape to get approval. So instead, I created a fictitious talk show host, one equally as famous and just as wonderful as the real Oprah. The stories were pouring out in no particular order, meandering from decade to decade, story to story.

Somewhere along the way, I realized that these life stories had become about me – and – ering. In fact, the original book title was Me and Erings, as it was a literal account of all my *meanderings!* My talk show host became Erings B. Skye, the powerful, larger-than-life icon of daytime talk TV who could make anyone's dreams come true, merely by giving them a place to be seen and heard once—by the masses.

It may sound like an unusual way to tell your story, but for me it became increasingly realistic with every imaginary conversation I had with her. This dialogue went on day after day, week after week, silently of course, if only in my thoughts. When I finally got to the retreat, we were told that what we thought we were going to write might not be what came out. But for me, it was already crystal clear. The book practically wrote itself. So here you have me, the real-life Beverley Golden, telling my stories to the fictional talk show host, Erings B. Skye. I trust it all makes perfect sense!

Some may see my storyline as impossible or implausible. In fact, I've been asked why I would choose to present my story in a scenario that is half real, half fictional.

My answer: "Why not?" As Einstein said, "Reality is merely an illusion, albeit a very persistent one." Throughout my life I have been motivated by the word *impossible*, because I choose to live in a world of unlimited possibilities. I haven't always been that way, as you'll find out. My life has been what I often call *a journey to possible*, with lots of resistance along the way.

As you will also discover, I have traveled a long and often lonely road of choices that literally no one else agreed with, especially regarding my physical health. That's because I learned, early on, to always stand on my own, trusting what feels right to me. My lifelong quest has been to lead an unconventional life, and through sharing the experiences I've had on the roller coaster ride of life, to offer others hope that it's possible to do the same. And the title word *confessions* is used in perhaps a bit of an unconventional way, too. It is about me admitting to my strengths and weaknesses, the challenges and triumphs that come from being human.

A wise teacher taught me that reading sometimes requires "the willing suspension of disbelief"—and while writing *Confessions*, I realized that meant: let go of the need for the story to be 100 percent logical and see what comes to you—what insight you might take from it! So although a conversation between a living person (yours truly) and a fictional talk TV diva may seem impossible, I invite you to step outside the realm of plausible and look at Erings as the personification of your own listening ear, or even as the silent listener in "every person." Because at the very heart of it all, Erings is you! She is the ever-curious listener in a long and winding conversation. She embodies all the teachers, healers, practitioners, coaches, respected gurus, friends and family and even the doctors and business associates who have all been there to support and listen to me throughout my unfolding life stories, often becoming integral parts of them.

We all have unique and fascinating lives, if we choose to look at them that way. My father was an incredible storyteller, although he told mostly other people's stories. For as long as I can remember, it seems I've always been like my father in that way, too. I've been called a word magician, a person who can communicate ideas and wisdom to others simply through the stories of my life experiences. At heart, I'm a dreamer, a dream weaver, who silently observes the world and then creates stories that I hope everyone can relate to.

So be forewarned: this book is in no particular chronological order. Similar to the way our minds flow in streams of consciousness, it meanders from decade to decade and then back again. One chapter, I'm a child and the next I might be giving birth. Then I'm back to my wedding day or the day I met my husband. Past, present and future intertwining and connecting in this moment. It all makes perfect sense to me. Life in a chronological sequence seems static and a bit boring. This book is an unconventional way of telling my story and I invite you to dive in and swim along with me.

It's always challenging to know when a book is really finished. It feels like this book is part of a work in progress, just as my life is. I trust that the stories that emerged in my head during those winter walks, and then poured onto the page at the retreat, are exactly the stories that you're ready to hear. Or at the very least, the ones that I need to express.

There are many other stories I could have included here, and I believe there are many more to come. Every day of my life, in fact, I view as another story waiting to be told. Perhaps the most important story is the one that tells you that I am in fact still here, to even tell these stories. In looking back, I'm amazed at all the things *I didn't do* that I was told "I must do" to survive. In fact, more often than not, I did what appeared to be diametrically opposed to my "best interest," throwing caution to the wind and abandoning better judgment. I'd like to attribute it to my absolute trust in my intuitive Aquarian contrarian visionary ability, combined with my knack for pulling ideas seemingly out of thin air and bringing them down to earth to experience in a rather offbeat way. The real truth, though, is that I honestly feel *I've been guided* to inject even the darkest of moments with hope and humor, and then to share them with others to offer another way to look at life.

Before we begin, I must express my sincere thanks to all the players in my story. Without you, there are no stories at all. With some of you, I honestly have no idea where life has led you since our paths crossed. If you recognize yourself, I would love to hear from you. To others who are still part of my story, I am grateful to have you in my life. I've consciously and purposely left out names, wherever I could. My immediate family is no big secret…so you appear, names and all.

Thank you for stopping by to be a new part of my life, an ongoing journey continuing to unfold. May this book, and all that might happen because of it, spark the stories that will populate and become the next chapters of each of our wonderful lives.

As I always say…to be continued.

In the Beginning

"There is very little hope for healing on a physical level. All we can offer you is that perhaps you should pray." It had been a long road back, and boy, had I proved those doctors wrong. Memories raced through my mind as I caught a glimpse of the now smiling, vibrant and healthy me in the full-length green room mirror.

I felt almost overcome with sheer joy, knowing that all my stubborn Aquarian contrarian persistence, plus trust in my never-ending inquisitiveness and intuition, had brought me back, literally from the living dead. Having survived against all the odds, I was now fully present and able to stand in this place. Ready and willing to finally tell my story and perhaps share some hope and humor that might inspire, uplift and shake up a little bit of the complacency in the world around me.

I snapped back into the moment as the production assistant's booming voice filled the air with eleven words that made my heart skip a beat: "Five minutes until author Beverley Golden is up. Are you ready?" Was I ready! Again, I felt overcome, but this time by silent, internal, uncontrollable laughter. For me, this was a very private joke. It seemed I had spent my entire life getting ready for *this* exact moment.

So where was I? Backstage and about to be interviewed by Erings B. Skye, the international media tycoon whose top-rated syndicated talk show was THE place to be seen and heard by any aspiring first-time author's standards. It promised to be a long interview, as Erings wanted me to share my whole story. It would be divided up into segments, as her producer had explained, and then broadcast as a continuing series over the next few months.

Judging from the excitement of the previous guest who had just returned to the green room, I sensed how comfortable Erings had made him feel and I became curious if all I had heard about her was true. Like a computer, my mind began to scan all I remembered or had researched about Erings B. Skye in preparing for today.

The product of a late-in-life birth, Erings was the only child of parents who had desperately wanted children. From the beginning of her life, she was treated like their special little princess. Her astronomer father and stay-at-home (amateur astrologer) mother had been thrilled and overjoyed at her arrival. After almost giving up all hope of having a child, she brought them a joy beyond words.

Erings loved books and was reading by the age of three. She loved animals and it appeared that she was genuinely sensitive, kind and loving to everyone. Somehow I had drawn many parallels to my own early life. I too had loved books, read from an early age and adored animals. Sometimes I thought the word "sensitive" must have been invented especially for me as a child.

Erings, the woman, had been in a committed relationship for a very long time, but had no children of her own. "All the children of the world are my children" was her mantra. She had donated or raised millions of dollars for children's causes, from health care in third world countries to helping to build schools for young girls so that they could rise to their full potential through education. Over the years, Erings' name had become synonymous with empowering people to reach for the sky and to dream their greatest dreams.

No one knew for sure what or where her name came from—Erings. Rumors surfaced, from time to time, that her name was really Erin and the 'GS' was added by her parents to give her a completely unique name. There was no one else in the world with her name! The extra letters were reported to stand for God Send. Her parents had been liberal, creative and open-minded, yet the thought never crossed their minds that giving their daughter such an unusual name would create this constant conversation and speculation.

It was also rumored that the mysterious middle initial 'B' stood for Blue. This was never confirmed and often unsolicited stories about her would refer to her as Erings Blue Skye. Erings herself did not care to talk about her name. She had made a practice of taking the focus off herself to ensure the spotlight was pointed on what she believed was most important—her guests and their issues.

For millions, if not billions, of people whose lives she continued to inspire, she was like a little bit of heaven entering their living rooms daily. Her syndicated talk show and her company *The Skye's The Limit* could either make or break those who were hoping to be seen, those hoping to find a platform and have a voice.

Erings B. Skye had the power to make that happen. A phrase, "The E Effect," was coined in reference to her continued ability to create magic for those whose lives she touched. Even if you weren't graced to land a spot on her television show, having your book mentioned in her magazine, or selected for her book club, also seemed to guarantee success. Some reported that it was like being catapulted from obscurity to overnight fame in the blink of the eye. Erings was always surprised to hear this. She never used her power in any way that would look like she favored someone or stacked the deck.

A champion of personal experience, she truly loved to support anyone or anything that struck a chord in her own heart. From entertainment to politics to the publishing world, Erings offered the worldwide stage that was her talk show with an integrity and honesty that people trusted. She was like everyone's friend and universally considered to be "the real deal." Compassionate, engaged, informed and loving, Erings instilled confidence in those around her. If she believed it was possible, maybe it was.

So here I was, feeling overcome by the synchronicity that had led me to this moment. It was like some cosmic force had moved all the pieces of my life's puzzle into place. I was nervous. In a good way. When I caught myself not breathing, I remembered—in and out. *In...and...out.* This was it. In less than five minutes, I'd be on international television. Maybe those dreams of fame (and fortune) were minutes from coming true.

How did I get here? A lifetime captured in a simple book had somehow caught the attention of the right people, in the right place, at the right time. Amazing how trust and divine intervention work together sometimes! The angels were watching over me for sure, guiding me to this place in this precise moment. I know that there are no accidents. I thought of Einstein and his words: "Synchronicity is God's way of remaining anonymous."

Out of the blue, my mind started racing full speed again. What stories would Erings talk to me about? The funny ones, the quirky ones, the educational ones, the sentimental and uplifting ones—or would they unfold, as they had in my book, in random order? Would they even sound funny? Some of my life was so very serious, but I always tried to infuse a rather offbeat, humorous slant.

Would Erings ask about the early memories or the more current stuff? I knew I was prepared. How could I not be? After all, it was my life! Suddenly I panicked, thinking that maybe Erings wouldn't ask me about any of the funny stuff. Since when had the funny stuff become my obsession? Breathe. In and out. This life I had lived, it had so many lows but also lots of highs. The roller coaster ride of life. I loved every minute of it. My main theme: health. I had been told that my story gave people hope. Continuing to defy the odds, taking a road not recommended over and over again, I was here to tell my story. I had been told repeatedly that I was a paradigm shifter, changing perceptions about what was possible relating to physical health and healing. Always motivated by the *impossible*.

While I was lost somewhere else in time, the memories were flooding not only my mind, but every cell of my body. Dancing like liquid lava inside my heart. I was traveling to other places, a long ago time. To a "me" I probably wouldn't even recognize now, if I met her back then.

I snapped into the present moment again, as I saw, then heard, the production assistant coming back into the green room. This time, it was to get me. She announced that there were two minutes until Beverley's introduction.

Some crazy notion that each life unfolds like a tapestry, or an intricate work of art, zoomed through my mind. The streaming, seemingly random thoughts continued. How each life is so individual as it continues to change and grow. "Let go of the philosophy, Beverley," I silently instructed myself. How exactly was this relevant right now? I trusted the very fact that I'd survived and had mustered the courage to write my story was reason enough for me to be here. Yet, I caught myself thinking, "I really hope I don't blow it."

Breathe…in…and…out.

With about thirty seconds to go, I heard Erings' baritone voice giving a brief introduction of her next guest and why she had asked her (which was me) to be on the show, explaining that this was the beginning of a series of segments. I looked up and caught site of her in the monitor as she told the audience she was willing to devote as much time as it took to let me tell my story. "That, in itself, is something I've actually never done before," she said with a big smile on her face. This declaration to the world made me even more nervous than I ever thought I would be. So many stories to tell…would there really be enough time?

Finally, it was the moment I'd meet Erings B. Skye, the famous full-bodied woman with a big, warm voice and an even bigger heart. I inched toward the sea of blinding studio lights and what sounded to me like thunderous applause. Had the audience read my book? Okay. I couldn't imagine who knew about me other than those closest to me, those who had lived their lives by my side. Well, maybe a few other people, too.

As I stepped out from behind the curtains, I glimpsed the steps before me and almost floated down them. Standing inches away, face to face with Erings, seemed almost too much to bear. My heart skipped several more beats. I realized I was again holding my breath. I centered myself, coming back into this moment. "Get out of your head, and back into your body," I silently commanded myself. I was here. I had arrived.

Erings asked me to take a seat, looked me in the eyes and said, "I'm so happy to have you here, Beverley. I found reading your book *Confessions of a Middle-Aged Hippie: Observations of Life on Earth and Other Cosmic Meanderings* both fun and captivating. Yours is an intriguing story that leaves us *all* open to look at our own lives from a bit of a new perspective."

I sat there, stunned. In total awe.

"Love the title, by the way," Erings threw in as an aside.

I think I said, "Wow. Thank you so much!" in an amazed and surprised voice. Very profound reply, yes? Shaky for sure. Was this my voice? Was I audible? I had always been so comfortable talking in front of people. *Do Not Lose It Now!*

I was overwhelmed. Flying high on an adrenaline rush. The phrase "sheer bliss" came to mind. My body was tingling. My heart felt ten stories high. My smile (which probably looked moronic) was so wide my cheeks hurt. I hoped no one would notice.

I was really, finally here. Simply because of who I am.

Who's Your Daddy?

Erings: Well, I personally am very, very excited to have you here, Beverley. I must tell you that while reading your book, I found myself laughing and crying—sometimes at the same time. I was truly touched by your journey!

Beverley: Thank you. I am incredibly honored and humbled to have been invited here to talk with you about my book, about my story, my life. I'm generally a highly private person, so sharing my life, first in my book, and now here in front of...

Erings: (smiling) Probably millions of people.

Beverley: Yes, that is *very* big for me for sure. A little bit overwhelming and surreal.

Erings: May I say that sometimes while reading your book, Beverley, I had to remind myself that these stories actually happened.

Beverley: I should say thank you for that, because often real life is stranger than fiction could ever be. A big part of what makes my stories fiction-like is my signature way of observing each event, then creating a running commentary, which I can only hope might make people laugh.

More often than not, my self-deprecating humor saves me. It's generally much after the fact, though, because in most of my darkest hours, things looked very bleak indeed. Physical pain is a great leveler.

Erings: So what would you say it is, in you, that allows you to come through these dark times and still be able to find the humor in them?

Beverley: I honestly don't know for sure, Erings. I've often heard that people use humor to cope. So maybe my warped worldview helps me in that way. I definitely see humor in a quirky, offbeat way. Often in places where others don't even see it. I find it in virtually everything. I know when I can take a step back and observe— for me that's how it all replays itself out…with humor.

I also have a really strong will, plus a rather loud sense of intuition. I've learned over the years not to ignore it. Whenever I trusted that inner intuition and really listened, I always made the right choices for myself.

Erings: I get that you have often gone against the "better advice" of everyone around you, be they family, friends or even doctors.

Beverley: (smiling) I do confess. That is definitely who I am. As an Aquarian, like you Erings (although I can't 100 percent confirm this is true of all Aquarians), I generally do go against the grain or the norm. I ask lots and lots of questions, because that is how I take in the overall big picture. I assimilate all the information and somehow throw out what I don't need, use what I do need, and come up with the perfect choice for myself.

Many times, especially when I was critically ill and not expected to make it, I astounded mostly everyone, took the most unconventional route and somehow came out ahead.

Erings: Yes, I got that from reading your book. First of all, I guess I should set the geographical stage and ask, where were you born and where are these stories or events unfolding?

Beverley: I was born and still live in Toronto, Ontario, Canada. Other than when on trips or traveling, the majority of my life has happened on home soil.

Erings: Thanks for that. I can hear some of the Canadians in the audience cheering their support.

There are so many things I'd love to ask you about. I almost don't know where to start with someone with your kind of story.

Beverley: I can have that effect on people.

Erings: (laughing) Well, my first instinct was to begin at the beginning, but with someone like you, it almost seems too obvious. Hmmm. Okay, why not go for the obvious, because your beginnings really do perfectly set the stage. From what I read, that mystery surrounding your birth helped define who you would become.

Beverley: Absolutely. It seems I've told this story hundreds of times before and always thought I'd finally and completely worked through it. However, every new time brings up another layer of the onion that wants to be peeled back and healed. This part of the story, in movie terms, is "the setup." And just to warn you all, this is definitely *not* the humorous part. So here goes.

Two years before I was born, my mother was married to her first husband and they had a child (a boy) whom she had carried full term and then who died three hours after birth.

Erings: Wow. Although I don't have any children of my own, I cannot even imagine what that must have been like for your mother. To carry a child to term and then to lose it just like that.

Beverley: As you'll come to hear, my mother is incredibly strong. Solid like a rock. Although she is a Pisces, her moon is in Aquarius and this gives her a detachment that helps her survive emotionally. At this moment, she is ninety-seven and is still going strong, although she has definitely slowed down in the last year.

She still lives on her own and is the social butterfly of the community. My mother truly loves people and is a charming and likable person. She's the lady who is like everyone's mother or grandmother. She's the one who offers her shoulder to cry on. She's tough, but still soft and caring.

This first marriage was a very unhappy one for her. She had been planning to leave it and was at the time having an affair with my father, who was the guy upstairs, also in an unhappy marriage. She got pregnant with me and decided to stay in the first marriage, mainly because in 1949 you didn't just up and leave. As it was, she was harshly judged by those around her when the news of the affair surfaced and she did finally decide to leave him.

Erings: So are you saying she stayed in the marriage?

Beverley: She did. When I was born, weighing in at 9 pounds 11 ounces (who would ever imagine my birth weight would be a numeric code for trouble), she named me after someone in his family who had died and continued to let him believe I was his child. In the Jewish tradition, children are named after someone, generally a relative, who has passed away. It is to honor their name and let it live on. Here I am, starting my life named after some male relative of someone I'm not even related to.

Erings: So, the first husband thought you were his child?

Beverley: Yes, he did. It was a very delicate, yet tough situation. My mother stayed with him for one and a half years until she felt it was the right time to leave him. She was brave enough to leave everything actually, and move us in with her sister and family for the next year.

This was a pivotal time in my life I now see, because my mother's sister became like a second mother to me. My mother had to go out to work, I think in a dress factory and then as a bookkeeper, and my aunt was the one who looked after me during the days, during the year we lived there.

Erings: So when did you find out about this man who thought he was your father?

Beverley: I do remember visiting with this man at times, but my mom had married my real birth dad when I was two and a half, and we became a happy family.

The divine timing was that when I was four, my brother, Niel, was born. Right around that time, the first husband, who thought he was my father, died very suddenly of a heart attack. So now, he was conveniently out of the picture. For some reason, my parents thought it best to keep the story from me and my mom didn't actually tell me until I was twelve.

Erings: Twelve?

Beverley: I know that familiar reaction all too well. For a lot of my childhood, I thought I might be adopted, because I would receive these gifts on holidays and birthdays, yet wasn't told who they were from. There were also hidden papers in my mother's bedside drawer. I discovered them by accident one day and had no idea what they were. For some reason it made me question if I was adopted. When I asked about this, I was told I was being silly or ridiculous.

Later in life I was told by a chiropractor, who'd asked me if I was adopted, that I had a pattern in my neck he often saw in adopted children. Not sure what exactly that felt like to him, but I know I still get jammed in the right side of my middle neck. I still hold tension there.

Erings: This is obviously a sensitive and emotional issue for you.

Beverley: Yes, and it is just one example of how these early life situations, and the impressions they make, can leave a lasting imprint physically. Even though I was not adopted...I truly wondered and maybe even believed that I was.

My mother finally decided to tell me the whole story when I was twelve. It was June 1961 to be exact. A beautiful, sunny day. I remember it clearly. I actually have a vivid recollection of something in me closing off the moment she told me. I understand now that I shut down on a very deep physical level in my solar plexus, which I later learned has to do with identity; it's the region of your body that literally symbolizes your core and who you believe you are. This is also the digestive area of the body and when we can't digest things in our lives emotionally, we might develop issues with our physical digestive system.

Erings: So let me clarify. The area of your body that shut down was related to who you are and played out as a digestive issue?

Beverley: The simple answer for me is yes. Maybe other people have different ways of reacting. For me, it has always been about the digestive system. I realize that I couldn't digest the information my mother was telling me.

Erings: Can you tell us what might have been going on for you that allowed this to happen this way?

Beverley: For whatever reason, in the moment she told me, the word "tramp" came into my mind (relating to my mother). I was so shocked, I didn't know how I could trust anything she had ever said. Let me say here that I loved my mother and had always clung to her. As much as she smothered me with her sheer delight at having a child to love, I smothered her, too. I adored her. But, this information, at this formative age, was beyond my understanding. Simply put, I just couldn't digest it.

Erings: Did this change your relationship with your mother?

Beverley: If it did, I wasn't conscious of it then. I still adored, loved and mentally trusted my mother so much, despite my heart's uncertainty if I could ever believe her again. I had been so attached to my mother that I would throw a tantrum if she tried to leave the house. She actually could not leave the house until I was five years old, unless I was asleep. I was very clingy in lots of ways. I sucked my thumb until I was almost five as well. I had this blanket that I clung to and would never let go of. The only time my mother could wash the blanket was when I was asleep.

Erings: Sounds like you were very close to your mother before this.

Beverley: Yes, I had always been by my mother's side. Possibly on an unconscious level, I had made her my security, only feeling safe when she was around. In fact, my first memory of me, as an "I," was when my mother was pregnant with my brother. We were out for a walk, holding hands as we always did, but she was so large, she literally fell off the curb and landed on her belly on the side of the road! I clearly remember panicking and thinking, "I can't help my mother."

Although that was true, luckily, a lovely knight in shining armor (in the form of a stranger) came to our rescue, helped her up and made sure she was okay. I was terrified, crying and screaming, "Mommy, mommy, are you okay?" My brother was born the next day. I hope you can understand why this story my mother told me at the age of twelve mortified me, to say the least.

Erings: And is this where your health issues began?

Beverley: Yes and no. Yes, as the obvious answer, but as a child I believe there were also early warning signs. I was highly sensitive, allergic to orange juice as a baby. I am often reminded that I was a very serious child who didn't smile a lot. Generally though, I didn't have an early childhood plagued by illness. Just the typical things…measles, maybe mumps. I was an intense student from an early age as well. Being somewhat shy, I preferred sitting in a corner reading or observing, but I don't have memories of ever actively engaging in play.

I was also a clean freak, even at three or four. Any time I would get dirty, I'd demand that my mother change me, so I would be clean again. She laughs about how she would indulge me and sometimes change me six times a day. I really didn't like getting down in the dirt, as they say, with other kids. But, I could read fluently from about the age of four and loved to read out loud to anyone who would listen, including my kindergarten classmates. I'm sure that my teacher, wherever she is, would testify to my early love of words and ideas and sharing them with others.

Erings: That story about your first day of kindergarten confirms the "clingy" you for sure. It is surprising that you have such a very clear memory of it, actually.

Beverley: Yes, clingy I was…and a burgeoning drama queen as well. I sure had learned how to get attention. I was a little bit older than others in the typical kindergarten class, because my birthday is in February. On that first day, my mother walked me to school and although I can't officially remember if I'd planned it, I was kicking and screaming, crying all the way. I remember breaking into full-blown tantrum mode at the classroom door. I clung to my mother for dear life and would not let go, no matter what she said. By this time, the teacher had come out to greet me. That definitely didn't help. I cried. I screamed. It was painful for both my mother and the teacher, their encouragement aside.

Quickly, an emphatic "leave her—she'll be alright" came from the teacher. This was my first drama-queen tantrum. I remember looking up and seeing my mother peering through the small window of the closed classroom door. I was in committed acting mode as the teacher continued encouraging me to join the class, while waving at my mother to walk away. Mine was a verbal cue. My mother's cue, a shooing of the hand.

Erings: It sounds dramatic for you, your mother and the teacher. What was the outcome?

Beverley: I kept looking up at my mother with my irresistible, teary, puppy-dog eyes and pouty frown. I made it so difficult for her to leave. I do remember that the minute she left, when the window was clear, I stopped the crying and marched right into the middle of the group of my newfound peers, instantly adopting the classroom as my new home away from home.

I loved the stimulation of the colors and the numbers and everything new and exciting that kindergarten offered me. Before long, I was immersed in classroom life and it only supported my love of learning. From the very beginning, I adored school. To this day, I still adore school and learning. I have been a non-stop, perpetual student and I keep going back for more. When it comes to school, I could never get enough.

I see now, I wasn't a very daring student—I always colored inside the lines. I was perhaps too rule oriented, too rigid. However, for me, school was like being in heaven. I loved my year in grade two the most. I had this beautiful young teacher who seemed to favor me, along with one other student, my main competition for her attention. The two of us were continuously vying for the teacher's attention, as she would give out stars for top marks in spelling and math.

Although I was very gifted in those two subjects, my competitor was a burgeoning artist. I still remember how her tongue would hang out to one side when she was drawing or painting. I always hoped she would use her talents and become an artist. Although now I see that in many ways *I* was actually always an artist, too. I learned to nurture that part of myself as I got older.

My teacher was so caring that she even came to visit me in the hospital when I had my tonsils out. She had a way of making me feel special.

Erings: I certainly relate to your love of books and reading, as I also have adored them my whole life. But let's get back to the repercussions of you being told the "whole truth" when you were twelve years old. You described this as the real beginning of "my health downfall."

Beverley: Yes. Within a short amount of time, I was unable to hold food down and started to lose a dramatic amount of weight. I was in constant and chronic debilitating pain, yet doctor after doctor could not find anything wrong with me. Test after test, month after month, I was getting sicker and sicker. At my lowest point, I was extremely malnourished and down to about 85 pounds. The doctors were baffled and told my parents that it was all because I was a perfectionist. Although this was true, I'm absolutely sure that perfectionism was not a legitimate diagnosis.

After all this time spent on highly invasive tests, nothing showed up. The entire process was proving fruitless, which took its toll on not only me, but my whole family.

Somehow, my body had delayed puberty. I may have been underdeveloped physically, but I was overdeveloped in the smarts area. Intellectually astute, but really far from street smart. I was one of the most naïve teens ever, I think. For example, when I had heard that Mia Farrow and Frank Sinatra were a couple, I remember thinking that they couldn't possibly be sleeping together. Only loose women had sex with…well, whomever. So, when my mom told me my story at the age of twelve, I shut down completely. I disconnected my head from my body. For years I walked around like this—a giant, overdeveloped head and an extremely underdeveloped body.

Erings: Yes, tell that part about the memory you have relating to this head and body issue, as it is truly fascinating.

Beverley: Well, for a lot of my life I really had no connection between my head and my body. They remained very separate parts of me. Sometime in my twenties, I had the thought that I was this wonderful, beautiful head, yet I was continually having to drag around this body. To elaborate, I believed it was too bad because it would be easier if I didn't have to take this body with me.

It is upsetting to actually have to acknowledge this, even though it sounds and seems ridiculous to me now. I was always "the pretty one" and "the smart one" — notice how both descriptions are based on the face and head.

Erings: I bet the therapists out there are gasping!

Beverley: I must clarify, because I spent a lot of time living with pain in my body during these years of my life, it did make some sense that just being in my head would be so much easier. I never had any real pleasurable experiences in my body.

It was a major disconnect—and quite real to me. I felt like this beautiful head with this really unattractive (to me only) body. Being in a physical body meant being in pain. Even now, I would say that very little pleasure has come to me through this body.

Erings: Really! Not even...

Beverley: Not really. (smiling) Until very recently. For many people, that can be a result of living in your head too much. Also, being in chronic physical pain makes you want to retreat, and for me, that meant shying away from physical contact and developing overexaggerated mental capabilities.

In my astrology chart, six planets are in air. That would almost predispose anyone to being up in the air, or overly caught up thinking and in the head. Being an "idea person" is a benefit, but living only there obviously leads to other consequences. Once again, Erings, I have somehow digressed.

Erings: That's okay. I'm starting to understand that your meandering storytelling style is what keeps us engaged. So, what happened next?

Beverley: Thank you and yes, what happened next. Finally at age twelve— November 22, 1963, to be exact—the day President John F. Kennedy was shot, my father picked me up from school and told me "the news." The doctors had finally found something. I would need to have surgery to fix a twist in my bowel. They all made it sound like it was just a minor operation and I would be okay after that.

In December 1963, the Christmas holiday marked the time for my "fix it up" surgery. The Beatles had just entered the consciousness of North America and the British Invasion was sweeping the nation. There were a lot of things I wasn't told, because there were a lot of things my parents weren't told. I hadn't started asking questions yet and just trusted my parents, who trusted the doctors. I think the promise of relief from pain, coupled with the prospect of good health again, overshadowed any questions or doubts any of us might have had.

Erings: Certainly understandable! How did the surgery go?

Beverley: Quite well. The surgeons removed two feet of my upper small bowel (the jejunum), then stitched it back together and left three metal clips holding it in place. Of course, the doctors had never seen a case like mine before. The small bowel and large bowel had somehow twisted themselves in a way that was so unusual, it was worthy of being written up in a prestigious medical journal. I love it. Fame for all the wrong reasons.

Erings: Well, although the surgery was successful, it sounds like this story isn't quite finished yet.

Beverley: Very true, Erings. The most devastating memory, which still lingers as the strongest of all, is waking up with a tube in my nose and down my throat. Why hadn't anyone told us about this? I'd say that this moment birthed the "asking lots of questions" part of me. No one ever again touched me before I could know every last detail of what to expect. I still remember pleading, in horror, to take out the tube. PLEASE! Unfortunately in those days, generally, no one listened to a kid.

I don't blame my parents, because at that time I was critically ill. People just trusted doctors to have all the right answers. Times have changed, so I strongly encourage everyone who finds themselves in the role of a patient to ask as many questions as they need to, so that they are 100 percent comfortable in knowing what to expect. No surprises! That's one of my health mottos.

Erings: That is wise and empowering advice for us all.

Beverley: Yes, well, this first surgery literally cut me up and made me question what else is possible. It was also the start of walking a new path and embracing another way of being a patient. "What else do I need to know?" is a question that must be asked until you feel ready to proceed. Now, I always ask, "Is that the only thing you have to offer?" If the answer is yes, I begin to look elsewhere, as I've learned there is *always* another way. Always. I'm a researcher at heart and that, combined with my strong belief in holding onto hope at all cost, propels me do something about it.

Erings: There is a positive takeaway in that for us all. Perhaps the road less traveled is something you'd encourage us all to at least try once in our lifetimes.

Beverley: I absolutely would. Trust yourself and follow your intuition.

Erings: When we return for our next segment, we'll talk about another trying time for Beverley. Another agonizing choice that doctors forced her to make… with humor, of course.

You're Having Your Baby... Tomorrow

Erings: We're back talking with author Beverley Golden about alternative versus conventional choices in medicine.

Now Beverley, in total, you have had four surgeries. So, I don't completely understand what you mean in saying you have chosen alternative over traditional medicine in your life. You continued to choose a conventional route, even after the first surgery at fourteen.

Beverley: That appears to be true on the surface. But, it's *how* I got to those choices that makes for the remarkable and often unbelievable stories. My most bizarre has to be my second surgery, when I was virtually forced to give birth to my daughter.

Erings: So, to set the stage, this story is more about conventional medicine and motherhood.

Beverley: Yes, it is about having to give birth early, through surgery. Incredibly and perhaps even dangerously early, in fact. It was a choice I never thought I would have to make. My daughter's expected due date was August 18th or 19th, which would have made her a late Leo, of course.

But about eight weeks early, I went into premature labor—after a minor fight with my husband—on Father's Day. We were totally unprepared! He and I were actually scheduled to start Lamaze classes the very next day. Instead, I was rushed to the hospital and a tremendous amount of effort went in to trying to stop this premature labor. It was all a blur of tubes and monitors and orders to remain still, quiet and calm. Then quite unexpectedly, my water broke—and I was told my only option was having my baby…tomorrow.

Erings: Get out!

Beverley: Believe me, Erings, I wanted nothing more than to get out. I had been in the hospital since Sunday. It was now Tuesday and my level of hysteria had grown disproportionately to the amount of time that had passed. It had been discovered in an ultrasound, that my child was lounging sideways in my belly. There would be no way to safely deliver her, other than a caesarean section. I immediately went into fighting mode. I'd never planned anything other than having a normal delivery.

That's when the scare tactics came out by the medical guys.

First, they brought in the head of obstetrics to deliver all the grim statistics to us. The doctor pulled everything you can imagine from his medical hat. I won't repeat the numbers here, but some of them were pretty convincing. Threats of serious lifetime diseases and complications can definitely terrify a new mother and father. Some of the hospital nurses very secretly and quietly told me not to do anything I was uncomfortable with, encouraging me to follow my own intuition.

When I called a trusted alternative heath practitioner for advice, she told me not to be "bamboozled" into a choice made for me by the medical doctors. At the time, although the word bamboozled felt extremely archaic, I immediately imagined the hospital doctors as hucksters ganging up on frightened first-time parents.

Even though I finally did succumb to the statistics, I had one last request of the specialists. With utter sincerity, I asked them if they could wait one extra day, because I didn't want to have a Gemini child. The extra day would allow the child to be born under the sign of Cancer. Made perfect sense to me. I'm sure you can imagine how well that request went over. The immediate response was, "If you don't take our advice on this one, we will have to withdraw from your case and you'll be on your own."

Now, really! Is that any way to treat a patient, I ask you?

Erings: So, you obviously didn't have any other choice *but* to have this second surgery.

Beverley: Correct, Erings. That was it. All discussions were over. The procedure was set for the following morning. A new Gemini was about to be born. Cut time set for 6:30 a.m. I had asked my personal medical doctor to be there, and on seeing his face, I felt some sense of comfort. "Do you think I am making a mistake?" I asked him. He had walked me through some pretty tough times in the last few years, so I absolutely trusted him.

In retrospect, I can't imagine he actually would have said, "Yes, Beverley, you are making a huge mistake." Especially not in the operating room! Anyway, he reassured me that after assessing the situation, he honestly believed that I didn't have any other options.

My baby girl was born on June 20, 1979, at 7:16 a.m., weighing in at 4 pounds 13 ounces. This was apparently a very good weight considering she was eight weeks premature.

Erings: Thank heavens! So tell us, how did the delivery go?

Beverley: The truth is that this whole episode was like a scene out of a "how not to give birth by C-Section" instructional video. It's amazing how something so simple can become a comedy of errors, or horrors, so quickly. My being in high-resistance mode complicated the situation for everyone. The normally simple procedure of putting an epidural needle in my spine made the experienced anesthetist look like an inept intern!

In the meantime, my husband, Doug, got all suited up in his doctor's garb, as we were determined to have him present during the birth. They had placed a sheet up to prevent him from seeing what was taking place on the actual cutting surface of my abdomen. He was permitted, with great reluctance by the medical team, to just stand beside me, be quiet and hold my hand. The scene was already spiraling out of control and he was as prone to hysteria as I was. Everybody present knew this.

Erings: Your visuals could inspire the script of a daytime TV movie. Tell us more.

Beverley: They had tried several times to stick that epidural in my spine and at this point, I wasn't sure what I could or couldn't feel. When they began to cut, vertically through my abdomen, I was positive that I felt something, so I screamed out in protest. They tried to calmly assure me I was FROZEN. I think that was a great way to describe my overall state in many ways.

I know that sometime, not long after the initial cut, the curtain that was shielding my husband from the vision of my open belly dropped. Within a split second, he fainted. As he fell to his knees and then the floor, someone was screaming, "Get him out of here!" I don't think he was officially escorted out, because the next thing I heard them say was, "It's a girl!"

Erings: Oh, wow.

Beverley: By this time, pink elephants were daintily pirouetting through my line of sight and I remember thinking, "A girl. Aww. I don't hear her crying. Is she alright?" I also wondered why these pink elephants were dancing. My husband was up and on his feet in time to hear her first tiny, goat-like cry. Baaaah. Even though it sounded so little, I was relieved to hear her announce herself to the world. Our new pediatrician proclaimed, "She's perfect!" as he whisked her into a waiting incubator.

Beverley at 9 months with mom, Lil ~ Beverley with Lani at 9 months
(Notice our identical no-hair look)

She was indeed perfect to us. Extraordinarily beautiful, as C-section babies often can be. She was completely bald…with a head so perfectly shaped, we called her little Nefertiti. The Egyptian Goddess. Her new home, the incubator, sealed her off from my world. We didn't know this at the time, but she would have to stay there for four incredibly long weeks.

Erings: Almost unbearable!

Beverley: That *and* I wasn't able to even touch her for the first few days. My incision had become infected after splitting open when I was walking down the hall to visit her in the nursery. It would have been too big a threat to the baby. So I was pretty much in hysterical mode for most of the first week, totally teary eyed, just longing to hold her. We already knew we'd name her Lani, which means "heavenly" in Hawaiian. We called her sweet Leilani.

Even other people, total strangers we didn't know, would stop at the nursery and comment on how beautiful she was. She was already entertaining people even at this age. Still, I was panicked that my beautiful little girl wouldn't bond with me. Although I had not even held her yet, against all odds, I refused to consider any possibility of *not* breastfeeding. Can you believe that I was discouraged from breastfeeding by the pediatrician? I thought, "Shame on all of them!" It was the only thing I had left to freely choose, considering the decision to have a natural childbirth was unexpectedly snatched away from me.

Erings: And now I know you well enough to realize you were not going to let it go!

Beverley: You got it. There was, however, one really important drawback to making this breastfeeding decision. One I had not seriously considered and no one made me aware of. Remember, we never got to attend a Lamaze class. So the one major drawback was that Lani had no sucking instinct, none whatsoever, having been born eight weeks premature. But I remained stubbornly adamant that I would breastfeed. Sheer determination. Lots of pumping. Lots of tenderness and pain.

Erings: Why were you so determined to breastfeed?

Beverley: Because I knew it was the best thing for me and for her. I guess that would be the expected answer. For me, the opportunity to defy incredible odds is the more honest answer as well. Another opportunity to turn impossible into possible. With the odds clearly stacked against me, I was determined to be successful.

Erings: But you were successful?

Beverley: I would say yes. May I admit and encourage others who want to give up that I did have to pump? And pump. And pump. I hear a few laughs out in the audience. I'm sure there are a few people here who can relate. I personally had to really, *really* pump to produce any milk. During the pregnancy, I had only gained 12 pounds and was accused, politely, of not eating.

Erings: But you had to be eating!

Beverley: Of course I was eating. The doctors even explored my bowel during the surgery but found nothing suspect or unusual. My blood tests showed an elevated platelet count, which can be an indication of inflammation. My OB/GYN was perplexed. Naturally, this is not the first time I had, or would perplex a medical doctor. After the birth, I gained more weight than during the pregnancy. An amazing 20 pounds, all of which were in my breasts. They got very, very large and heavy...two huge watermelons hanging on a wiry-thin vine.

I continued to persist through the pain, though. It seemed like I was always feeding my daughter. It was non-stop for two years. She had no regular feeding pattern and the pumping itself is very dehumanizing and painful. Of course eventually, I didn't need to pump anymore, except on special occasions.

Erings: Do you still think it was worth it?

Beverley: Absolutely. No question there for me. I preach persistence. One of the only problems was we could not get her to *stop* breastfeeding. Or to sleep. Ever. Doug's job required him to get up very early in the morning, so we had to put a bed in our dining room so he could sleep there. Interesting days.

Lani was definitely a late-night, no-schedule baby. At night I would bring her in to bed with me (as by this time, I had abandoned my plans to go back to work), so that I could feed her and maybe catch a moment of rest. She became quite accustomed to watching Johnny Carson with us. In fact, when she could talk, she was amazingly good at imitating Ed McMahon and his "Heeeere's Johnny" intro.

Lani also started calling her father "Dougie Boy." Somehow, people found this very cute and endearing and Lani was never shy to perform for people. We all love when people laugh with us and Lani was, and still is, a natural-born entertainer.

Erings: Cute. May I ask, how did you stop that pattern?

Beverley: When she was approximately twenty months old, I had the opportunity to become a partner in a too-good-to-be-true new business venture. We had to figure out a way to wean her from breastfeeding AND to get her potty trained at the same time. Otherwise, she wouldn't be allowed to go to daycare. Absolutely no leeway on that one. This proved quite the challenge.

She stubbornly refused to use the toilet. In fact, the only way we finally got her toilet trained was to promise her pretty pink frilly panties. It sounds pretty simple, but for some unknown reason, it worked. First daycare, then…by the time she was two and a half, I had persuaded the Montessori school to accept her as their youngest student ever.

This child had become the center of our attention, and my mother's attention too, from the minute she was born. She was, after all, an only child and an only grandchild. We never thought we were spoiling her though, as she was such a bright and well-behaved child.

Erings: In your book, you talk about how you weren't even sure you wanted a child and how you thought it might ruin your life. I found that surprising and wondered if it could possibly be true?

Beverley: I confess. True enough. I had actually said to my mother, "What if I don't love my baby?" She of course lovingly reassured me that I would. It does seem totally ridiculous in hindsight, but it is not the only ridiculous thing I have been known to say.

Erings: You also talk about the changes this brought about in your lives. Mind sharing?

Beverley: Well Erings, Doug and I had enormous dreams and envisioned ourselves making it in the entertainment industry. So, when I got pregnant, it was totally unplanned and unexpected. I was already twenty-nine, so in some ways the time was right. I had no idea what life would be like with a child and thought it would be the end of our careers. In many ways it was, because it changed our focus from us to her. An interesting bonus of parenthood.

Erings: (smiling) So your fears about being a mother were gone once you had your Gemini child?

Beverley: Yes. It is amazing how a child brings a new dimension into your life. Lani was an easy child, other than her perpetual breastfeeding. Actually there were never any terrible twos or whatever else people experience with their children. She didn't seem challenging in any way to me.

She was also very special from the beginning. Precocious, gregarious, charming. People stopped and were drawn in by this charismatic little being. She remains the same even today. I had always wanted a unique and unusual life for my daughter and that certainly is the way it played out.

Lani was a born performer. Maybe we fueled it by clapping for almost every single thing she did. She was noticeably talented at everything she tried. She knew, with certainty, from very early on, that she wanted to play the drums. So she did! She became a proficient percussionist before she was ten.

A cute story, I hope. When she was four, we took her to Sea World in Florida to see the whales and dolphins. She adored them. We were seated midway in the grandstand watching the incredible jumps and twists. Everyone was oohing and ahhing in amazement. After one particularly spectacular aerial jump, people started to applaud. Without a moment's hesitation, Lani jumped up and took a bow, convinced that the applause was for her.

(Looking over at Erings to catch her reaction, then out at the audience) I sincerely hope the therapists out there are *not* taking notes.

Erings: (smiling) I certainly hope not, too! It sounds like your life was enriched by this child, even though you had to face a second surgery to bring her into the world.

Beverley: Absolutely, Erings. I can't even imagine not having this incredible person in my life!

Erings: Two down and so much more to go. Join us for the next segment where we will talk about Beverley's next major health hurdle. A health issue that would derail an entire decade of her life.

The '80s –
Countdown to Number Three

Erings: So Beverley, you've made it to the early '80s. You are a contented new mother, but you talk about this period as being another challenging decade filled with extraordinary ups and downs for you. Most people have a year or two, yet you talk in decades.

Beverley: (laughing) I wouldn't do it any other way, Erings. And yes, the '80s, shall we say, was not one of my better decades.

I had started a partnership with a cousin and her husband in the newly emerging home video rental business. We were there in the very beginning, so there were no established ground rules for the industry as a whole yet. We were like pioneers exploring uncharted waters.

We called our store Videoflicks and it seemed literally within minutes, the business had taken off and people were approaching us about franchising. It was fast and frantic and exciting and we were in unknown territory. In fact, some movies, of the adult kind, were purchased from shady salespeople in dark parking lots, out of trunks of cars, late at night. It was the early days and as I said, there were almost no ground rules yet. But "adult movies," which we put in the separate monitored room in our store, were definitely a big part of the early home video industry.

I was an absolute movie fanatic—but because I did not like horror films, I was a bit concerned about having them in our store. Actually obsessively concerned. I feared the kind of person I might be forced to face. I wondered what kind of strange or demented characters rented horror films? In my imagination it wasn't the kind of people I now understand love this genre. To this day, I never watch that kind of film.

But I do still watch a lot of movies. It's one of my all-time favorite pastimes. Much of my early writing was actually for a national video magazine. I wrote feature articles on movie stars and in fact, a piece about Jimmy Stewart (unfortunately written under a pseudonym) received a wonderful reply letter *from* James Stewart himself, expressing his gratitude for the story. To quote the letter, which I still have: "I found it very interesting because it was different from many other things that have appeared over the years about me—and my wife, Gloria, thinks it's the best thing she's ever read."

Erings: How lovely. Must have been a very savored moment for you, Beverley. I must ask, do you have a favorite movie?

Beverley: It would have to be *A Wonderful Life*, ironically with Jimmy Stewart and Donna Reed. The message of that film resonates with me and my rose-colored-glasses sensibility. I have probably seen the movie fifty times, and every single time those last forty-five minutes get me. Each and every time. Without fail.

Erings: I would agree. Good choice. Now back to your business.

Beverley: Yes, our business was absolutely booming beyond any of our wildest expectations. Within several months, we were in full gear selling franchises and our flagship store was drawing people from unfathomable distances across the city. At that time, we could charge yearly membership fees, which were an amazing ongoing source of revenue. I was the spokesperson and we continued to generate lots of press and media coverage.

JAMES STEWART

April 24, 1986

Ms. Marisa Waldman
VIDEOMANIA
1314 Britannia Road East
Mississauga, Ontario L4W 1C8

Dear Marisa Waldman:

I want you to know that I'm very grateful to you
for the story you wrote about me in VIDEOMANIA.

I found it very interesting because it was different from many other things that have appeared
over the years about me -- and my wife, Gloria,
thinks it's the best thing she's ever read.

I send you my thanks and my best wishes.

James Stewart

JS/ap

Accolades for my writing from "the James Stewart"

The business was growing like spring wildflowers. We were definitely at the right place, at the right time, as the saying goes. As great as things appeared on the surface, I was experiencing a major decline in my health. Things at home were not very good. I understand, now, that our emotional health can have a direct and visible impact on our physical health. This was true for me. In this case not a good impact. It's the moon in Pisces in the sixth house. You astrologers out there will get that one. The sixth house has to do with well-being in relation to health and work. The moon represents your emotional self.

Erings: It's interesting to see you using astrological references for yourself to understand all the things that were happening.

Beverley: That is true, Erings. I'd say astrology has always interested me and I see the correlation between "as above, so below" in reference to how what is happening in the heavens is also affecting what happens to us here on Earth.

Erings: So how was it playing out down here on Earth for you?

Beverley: Well, I was dramatically losing weight and living with severe pain and chronic discomfort. My body was swelling with almost unbearable amounts of fluid. Although the business was a place of escape from my home life, the continued pressures from my partners were wearing me down. I ended up in the hospital.

A new, revered and God-like gastroenterologist entered my picture. This was supposedly the man you wanted to see if you were as sick as I was. He prescribed a battery of tests. My bowel was, to put it mildly, a mess. I certainly had a lot of experience ending up in hospitals unexpectedly. I often had ended up in different hospitals in the middle of the night. Memories were flooding back.

Many times, Doug and I showed up at our doctor's office, which was the house he happened to live in as well, in the middle of the night when I was in so much physical pain, I couldn't bear it another hour. Sometimes, this doctor would give me a Demerol shot, which successfully put me to sleep, giving my bowel time to relax and allowing me to wake up without pain. Not exactly the way to manage a disease, but that is often what I had to do. This night he was not there. We waited outside for a long time and finally my pain was so intense that after about six hours I really couldn't take it anymore. We decided I had to go to emergency.

I had lots and lots of experience with hospitals and emergency rooms, showing up in pain, explaining why I needed Demerol and inevitably being labeled as a drug addict. Or, at the very least there was often obvious suspicion. Refusal always signals suspicion. In one hospital they actually said to us that they don't dispense drugs to addicts. We were all dressed up in our stage clothes, so I hardly thought we fit the "addict" persona.

Erings: Really? Somehow I can't imagine anyone looking at you as an addict.

Beverley: Exactly. So here we are again, showing up at the local hospital, in emergency. Of course we explain the story. No go. They put me through extensive tests. I'm literally writhing in pain. It's been eight hours of excruciating pain by now. I remember one of the doctors coming down the hall toward me and almost screaming, "Get an IV in her, this woman is going to croak!"

Apparently, my hemoglobin level was only 48 and considering normal is between 120 and 160, this was considered deathly critical. I didn't even know how sick I was. I was working full-time and just continued to push myself.

So here I was, once again, in the hospital. Several days of rest and blood transfusions. I slept a lot. Again, everyone seemed worried, concerned I might not make it. I might want to add that for the average person, it is virtually impossible to be functional with a hemoglobin level of 48.

Erings: But, you're not average.

Beverley: (laughs) Yeah. That is true, but too often in this negative health-related way. Even I was afraid during this period. Of course I did make it, but people kept pushing me to find out what was *really* wrong with me. I was being told I couldn't go on like this. I was painfully aware of that, too.

The partnership was getting to the point where the word "tension" would be a mild way to describe it. I was feeling the pressure. They were, of course, concerned about my health and how it might have been affecting my day-to-day business performance. I was still working to maximum capacity. I had tried so many healing modalities, even a "nothing green" diet, which led me to eat tons of vanilla Häagen Dazs ice cream coupled with ridiculous quantities of popcorn, because both were white, not green. I sure had a way to justify my own interpretation of almost anything. I could make it work so it fit for me. It was hard for anyone to tell me otherwise.

Erings: Sounds like true Beverley…learning the hard way.

Beverley: I concede to that one, Erings. By now, my partners wanted me out. There was no more conversation about this. I don't know, even to this day, if their buying me out was the best or the worst thing for me. The business went on without me. Lots of my loyal customers missed me. But the financial compensation allowed me to go on and continue my healing journey as well.

I did go on to work in the video industry for the next three-plus years. I worked for a major distributor and then for a major video chain and after that for a major studio. My health continued to go downhill. I had even cut out my serious Diet Pepsi habit cold turkey. Nothing I did improved my health.

Erings: I see what you mean about this encompassing a lot of the decade.

Beverley: Yes, the decade is more than half over and I'm still searching. By 1986, I had already switched to a new gastroenterologist, as the other one had been too perplexed by me and wanted me to see a colleague who specialized in short bowel syndrome, which seemed to perfectly describe me.

Still, nobody could figure out exactly what was wrong. Speculation continued, but never anything definitive. Of course, drugs were always mentioned and I always, not so politely, refused.

This new gastroenterologist suggested I see a respected and cutting-edge (sorry for the pun here) GI surgeon, because there was a new form of surgery where they didn't have to remove anything. It had only been done on nine people to date.

It was called "strictureplasty" because they repaired, as opposed to removed, the strictures. I agreed to see him and found that I really liked his gentleness. He was confident, without a doubt, that my life would improve dramatically. I knew I had to do something, and this sounded like it was the something. I felt it would give me a chance. Frankly, I could not take the pain anymore or the disruption to my life.

Erings: And?

Beverley: In July 1986, I again went under the knife and had my third abdominal surgery. I had a total of seven strictures repaired. Surprisingly, they were spread throughout my bowel, not isolated in one part as they appeared in X-rays. I was convinced to go on prednisone (a corticosteroid, which doesn't build any muscle) and an immune suppressant.

Those "drug" years were horrible. I gained 40 to 50 pounds after the surgery. Almost it seemed, in the blink of an eye. I had so many symptoms from the drugs that I often wondered which was worse. Symptoms that not only had me gain a ridiculous amount of weight and develop a huge moon face, but ones that kept me awake at night, so hyper that at times I wanted to jump out of windows. I literally took to cleaning carpets in the middle of one night. It did seem like a wonderful way to use some of the excess energy. When I told my doctor, he asked if I could come to his house and clean his carpets. Good thing we both had a sense of humor!

Erings: Make them laugh. So this sounds like it was a wonderful choice for you.

Beverley: Yes, but also no. I still had episodes with my bowel and in the late '80s had to check myself into the hospital again, because I was so swollen with fluid that I couldn't walk. I was put on TPN (which is tube feeding via the chest) to bypass my digestive system and give it a rest. I lost 30 pounds of fluid in ten days. That is a lot of bathroom visits. I was actually told to stop urinating, because I was losing too much fluid too quickly. I virtually lived in the bathroom of my hospital room.

Erings: Sounds like quite another ordeal. Anything you can attribute that to?

Beverley: I think it was the trip to the Dominican Republic, and a subsequent feast of pork spare ribs bought from a roadside vendor, that might have led to me getting parasites.

(smiling) Of course no one knows for sure. With me, no one ever knows for sure. But, it is always about the gut for me. In my life, all my health issues always ended up being about the gut. The place of deep emotion and again, the gut is about who you are, your personal identity and self-esteem.

So, as you can see, the '80s were much more about sickness than health for me. Perhaps I'll end this particular life chapter here. I don't know what else I can say about the '80s. (smiling) Glad they're over, maybe. On a positive note, let me also add that it once again proved my resilience and ability to make choices for myself, even in the most dire of circumstances.

If I look at the events of this decade now, I would say that it continued to reaffirm for me that trusting myself and my gut (or intuition) was always the right choice for me. Although this decade was filled with its share of highs, it definitely had more lows and moments of complete despair. I would also have to say in many ways I came out stronger and a little bit wiser though. Definitely prepared for the next wave of challenges to come.

Erings: Okay. I'd say this is a great place for us all to take a deep breath. I'm going to take a short break. We'll be back and continue the conversation.

Erings leans over and speaks directly to Beverley: "Thanks. That sounds like it was a very tough time for you. I appreciate how well you handled the telling of it."

Love and Blizzards...Maybe Mother Nature Really Does Know Best

Erings: We're back after a particularly rough segment with author Beverley Golden. I'm going to switch gears a little bit and veer away from the last and final health episode until later. Let's move to an area I am very curious to hear more about: your days in the music business. I'd especially like it if you would start with the first time you met your husband Doug and then, of course, the day you got married.

Beverley: (smiling) Well, Erings, the first time I met my future husband Doug was an interestingly synchronistic kind of day. I now know it is extremely dangerous to go out on a first date in a blizzard with someone who happens to be extraordinarily tall, just because you want to go to a recording studio, to see what it is like. I was in the music business, working in show bands and as a lead singer in other cover bands, but I had never been to a real, full-fledged recording studio.

It was March 17th, 1973, a blizzard-like St. Patrick's Day. So, my date and I decide to head out in this blinding snowstorm to go to a local club to see a friend of his playing. Because there are hardly any people who have dared to brave the storm that night (I think we might be the only people), the upstairs and downstairs acts are playing together.

Sitting there in the dimly lit room, I find myself attracted to this very well-dressed musician who's performing up on stage; he's wearing a pink, flowing shirt and a burgundy velvet vest. His face is adorned, more like covered actually, with a massive beard, long hair and John Lennon glasses. It definitely wasn't the look I usually went for.

Beverley and Doug just after meeting, 1973

I'd never been as attracted to, or completely captured and curious about, a musician like this before. Or any man, musician or not. Somehow, in the eyes I was looking through then, he sincerely looked like an affluent musician to me. That was my first mistake. His demeanor was forceful and he sang incredibly loud, wailing at the top of his register in every song. In the long, dark room, we somehow couldn't keep our eyes off each other. I'm not sure what either of us could actually see.

Erings: So care to tell us what it was you "saw"?

Beverley: What I can say now is that we had an instant connection; we were drawn to each other and stayed together every minute of every day from then on. It didn't, however, take very long to find out that he wasn't affluent. He actually possessed very little. He was wearing stage clothes he had inherited from his stint as Judas in Jesus Christ Superstar. He had no underwear and only one pair of socks, which were purple. They couldn't be seen, as they were hidden inside his platform boots.

At the studio, he continued to compliment my eyes, but he was repeatedly vocal about the fact that he didn't like my earrings. Big '70's-type, mono-color balls sitting on my lobes. Randy Newman's album *Sail Away* was playing in the background and Randy has continued to be a favorite of both of ours throughout all these years, in spite of everything else.

Erings: I agree that Randy Newman is terrific. Hmm. Doug does sound... interesting. When you say you were together from that night on, I'm curious what happened to your date?

Beverley: Well, I believe I did go home with my date, who happened to be friends with the other musician performing that night. Because there were so few of us and everyone seemed to know everyone else, we all landed up back at the studio together. And yes, for whatever reason, it was Doug who really interested me, in spite of his bohemian style. He was totally and absolutely different from anyone this little, shy girl had ever met. Uncharacteristically different to say the least. Doug called me the next day and the rest, as they say, is history.

It was obviously our destiny to meet and to forge a relationship together. We quickly formed our own musical group called Billard and played together at times as a self-contained duo, expanding to a six-piece band when the gigs were there.

Soon after we met, he got a prestigious gig as the lead singer for a hugely popular Canadian band, Lighthouse, and travelled with them to the southern U.S. on tour. It was really hard being away from him and when he returned and that gig ended for him, we continued our careers—recording songs, pitching songs to other artists and just trying to make it in the unpredictable music business. For me, it was going to have to be either make it big, or don't bother and get out of the business.

Erings: So, that really is a prevalent theme for you: all or nothing.

Beverley: Yes, that is a theme I seemed to keep carrying around with me.

Erings: And, after a two-year courtship, you decide to get married.

Beverley: I'm not sure I would call it a courtship as much as a crazy, non-stop roller coaster ride that just happened to end in a decision to get married.

Erings: Tell us about the wedding.

Beverley: We were excited because we had chosen what we were sure would be a foolproof weather day. Nobody talked too much about global warming and weather in 1975. At least not people we knew. We were originally going to get married on March 17, the anniversary of the day we had met, but felt safer choosing April 6th.

Erings: Astrological reasons?

Beverley: Not so much astrological, Erings, as we anticipated how incredible early April would be. We had envisioned the perfect wedding, which would take place at my aunt and uncle's charming suburban house. We honestly never expected anything other than that. We cavalierly believed that everyone would be able to wear spring clothes and have no problem traveling and arriving from long distances.

But first, we had to find someone who would be willing to marry us. I am Jewish and Doug is not and he was not going to convert. We had heard about this rabbi who believed that any couple who wanted to get married should have that right. He had even gained a small amount of notoriety by flying to Las Vegas and performing a legitimate marriage ceremony for two Mynah birds. He got quite a bit of press from that one. We loved it!

Erings: Mynah birds? Really?

Beverley: Yes, and as far as we knew it was a true story. Who would make it up? It made for great press for the rabbi and we thought maybe even for us. I always loved an angle. We thought the whole thing was very funny and since we were anything but traditional, we were willing to hire him, if he was willing to marry us.

Erings: And?

Beverley: (smiling) Of course he was. Two musicians would be rather simple for him after Vegas and the Mynah birds. He probably wouldn't get as much publicity, but we were going to perpetuate the story into eternity. Thanks for the story, Rabbi Z.

As the day approached, we were getting more and more excited. Doug's mother, grandmother and two aunts were coming in from Halifax and we had a total of ninety-nine people who would be thrilled, delighted and happy to attend our wedding. That's what the R.S.V.P. cards had said anyways.

The day was fast approaching. I had found a beautiful, low-cut wedding gown, which I bought straight off the rack and knew would make great stage wear after the wedding. Doug and my brother had rented tuxedos. The food is ordered. The decorations in place. The rental glasses and dishes are about to arrive.

April had started with wonderful beautiful spring like weather. Boy, were we in for a huge surprise. Anyone who was actually living in 1975 might remember that a very unexpected snowstorm, a full-fledged blizzard had hit the eastern seaboard on April 4th and pretty much left life at a standstill.

Erings: Oh, yes. I do remember that.

Beverley: Years later, after researching that fateful day in our personal history, I found out that Bill Gates and Paul Allen had formed their little company, which they called Microsoft, on that very same day—April 4, 1975, in Albuquerque, New

Mexico. I remember thinking how lucky we all were that it didn't snow that day in New Mexico, as maybe the world of computers, as we now recognize it, would somehow never have happened.

Erings: Cool piece of synchronistic history. And for your wedding?

Beverley: For our wedding, not so lucky. People were snowed in and snowed out. My brother's car was snowed in up at York University and he had to hike out of the building he was in at the time so we could pick him up. Many people coming from out of town couldn't get out of their town, to come to our town. We were in no way prepared for uncooperative weather. We had to hustle some floor mats and coat racks to accommodate our guests and to save the front hallway of my aunt and uncle's house where we were having the wedding.

To make matters worse, Mother Nature blessed our wedding day with a blinding ice storm. We weren't even sure if anyone would be able to get there. Doug and the other men were literally carrying any guests who did arrive into the house from the street. The snow was very deep and the road conditions continued to be treacherous. The ice continued to pelt down.

The wedding party was getting more and more stressed out. Well, to be honest, it was really just Doug who was getting increasingly stressed out. I do remember thinking how glad I was that we hadn't invited the Mynah birds and that they didn't have to fly in from Las Vegas. Now, *that* would have been stressful.

At the last minute, it was decided by everyone, other than me, that my shoes, which were four-inch platform heels and very popular in the '70s, were in no way appropriate for the bride to wear. There is one lone picture of me in those crazy shoes and in retrospect they did look rather ridiculous. (The picture is now up on the back screen and there are lots of snickers and full out laughter from the audience, so Beverley stops to look at the picture too for a moment.)

Me, the vetoed wedding shoes, and my maid of honor, Sharon

I see you all agree. They do look quite ridiculous.

Erings: Yes, we all see what you mean and it sounds like many of the audience members just might recognize those shoes, too.

Beverley: (smiling) As well as those shoes, it was also decided for me that the décolletage of my wedding dress was cut way too low and showed way too much.

Quick fix. My cousin came to the rescue and found me some borrowed shoes—they were hers; she was younger and more conservative than I. I fought vehemently not to wear them, but I lost the fight. A really big, beautiful flower was also quickly shoved in my cleavage and everyone appeared to be happy again. (A new photo appears on the screen and the audience applauds.)

Wedding photo with flower-power décolletage, 1975

Erings: But something unexpected was happening, if I remember correctly.

Beverley: Yes, Erings, this happiness would be very short-lived. While we had been waiting for all the guests to arrive, something was happening that I didn't see coming. I wasn't made aware of it until the last minute.

It was now about thirty minutes before the actual ceremony and Doug very loudly started to accuse the photographer of taking too many pictures of *my* family and not enough pictures of his family. Everyone tried to calmly point out to him that he only *had* four family members at the wedding, but he was not going to have any of that. At times, logic did not work with Doug.

His yelling and screaming continued. With just thirty minutes until our wedding vows, both his mother and I are crying uncontrollably. My mother assured me that it was not too late to back out now if I wanted to. She never really understood the two of us as a couple. He was not what she expected me to choose as mate. The first time she saw him, she was visibly and vocally shocked. My mother never minced reactions or words. His mammoth beard and long hair were a little bit intimidating, I do admit. Kind of beast-like, actually. He always had a stoned look in his green eyes, too, come to think of it. I don't know if she ever really accepted us as a forever kind of couple.

At this point, even Doug's mother is telling me it's not too late to back out if I want to. Wow. What an omen. So I'm thinking, "I met him in a blizzard and now I'm marrying him in a blizzard. Maybe Mother Nature was trying to tell me something and I wasn't listening." Maybe I should have backed out, but being young and stubborn, I was willing to ignore the warning signs. Stubbornness had stopped me from backing out of many situations in my life. Someday I would learn. Apparently, this would not be that day.

Erings: Well, obviously you went ahead with it.

Beverley: Yes. Once eyes were dried and makeup touched up and pseudo apologies exchanged. I'm now ready, with borrowed shoes and covered breasts. Doug and my brother, who by the way had split open the back of his rented tux pants and is avoiding any unnecessary movements, are standing under the *chuppa*. This is a custom that symbolizes that the bride and groom are building a home together, and that it is always open to guests.

As is also custom, Doug is to break the glass, which is wrapped in a cloth—in this case a borrowed napkin—at the end of the ceremony. This really should have been a no-brainer because Doug was also wearing really thick, high platform boots. Remember, it was the 1970s. He was just lucky that no one could find a pair of suitable replacement shoes for him.

If you can, imagine this. The ceremony is almost over and Rabbi Z asks Doug to consecrate the vows by stepping on the glass. The breaking of the glass symbolizes that the marriage will last forever and never be broken, as long as the glass *is* broken.

What happens is yet another warning sign. Doug lifts his leg high for drama, steps down with great authority, but the glass somehow flies to the other side of the *chuppa* and with a quick, soccer-like save, my brother Niel, careful not to expose his butt cheeks, stops it with his shoe. He was wearing loafers, so his shoes might have in fact saved my marriage. He gently rolls it back towards Doug. Doug takes aim again, and Mazel Tov, the glass breaks. We're married!

We had now averted and survived two auspicious omens and our married life is about to begin. Of course, the rest of the night is a celebration of food and drink before it is time for the men to carry the guests back to their cars and for us to be off on our honeymoon. We weren't going on an official honeymoon, even though we had a hotel room booked.

Beverley and Doug finally married, cutting the wedding cake, 1975

Somehow my aunt thought that because nothing official was planned, it would be okay to ask if we could start our honeymoon by helping to clean up her house after the wedding. She wanted us to help stack the chairs and get the rental dishes ready for pickup. I have no idea why, but Doug said okay. So here we are, just married, and on clean-up duty after our wedding. The place was quite a mess and I was definitely not into it. It just didn't seem like the way to spend our first night as a married couple. Somehow it just didn't set the proper mood, if you know what I mean.

Erings: Hilarious story! You certainly never do things half way. We look forward to hearing more of your music biz stories and finding out about the stars you rubbed shoulders with in your travels. Let the conversation continue after this short break.

Jammin' and Searching

Erings: And we're back, talking with author Beverley Golden. I would love for you to tell the audience about the time you jammed with Rick James.

Beverley: Well, he wasn't "The Rick James" at the time. It was 1975, just after Doug and I had gotten married, and we were now performing with a larger band. We happened to be practicing with our group in a rehearsal hall. Someone knew a Buffalo-born singer and bass player who had defected to Canada and was playing with some local musicians in Toronto, including Levon Helms (The Band) and Neil Young.

Unbeknownst to us, they had invited him over to the rehearsal for an impromptu jam session. That singer was, in fact, Rick James. In he strutted, and in my memory, he immediately took control. We had decided, as a band, to tackle the song "Tell Me Something Good" by Rufus with Chaka Khan. They had already won a Grammy in 1974 for Best R&B Performance by a duo or group for this song. And the song was written by the incomparable Stevie Wonder. Would I even stand a chance?

I need to tell you that Rick James was the only black man in the room. We were a bunch of white musicians from the burbs. For me, this was *really* going to be a stretch. Rufus was an incredible band, and Chaka Khan was—and still is—a

legendary singer. I was more the "Cher meets Karen Carpenter" kind of singer...
and I was incredibly nervous.

The band was able to play the song perfectly. After all, it is easier for musicians
to capture the music than for this singer to capture the vocals. That's my take on
it, anyways. I'm singing it, but not-so-okay, when Rick James yells, "Sing it like
Chaka...sing it like Chaaaaaka!"

I looked around the room...no support there. I realized I'm the only singer in
the room who might have a chance to sing it like Chaka, being that I'm the only
female.

So I take a deep breath and go for it another time. Who am I fooling here? If
you know the song, the chorus goes: "Tell me something good"—low register,
that's easy cause the guys sing that—and then Chaka wails, I mean really wails,
"*Oh baby, baby, baby.*" Here I go, and in some oddly okay way, it kind of sounds
acceptable. If only to me. At least I wasn't totally embarrassed.

Erings: What did the others in the room think?

Beverley: That isn't something I remember, Erings, if I actually ever found out.
I still don't think Rick James thought I sounded like Chaka, but it is really a fun
memory for me. Of course, he went on to become the outrageous Rick James
later in the '70s with his 1978 dance song album *Come and Get It*, and then was
propelled to superstardom in 1981 with his song "Super Freak." Who knew at that
time that this might happen? He was just another musician trying to make it. Like
us all.

The only thing that happened to our band that even mildly related to Rufus or
Chaka Khan, was that our group went on to do a photo shoot where five white guys
and I took a group photo using almost the exact same pose that Rufus had used on
their 1974 album, *Rufusized*. I even got to wear my wedding dress in the picture,
without the flower, however. I always knew that dress would get to be worn the

proper way! And, I always loved that group picture. (The pictures are up side by side now on the large screen, and the audience members smile, nod, whistle and applaud in acknowledgment.)

Our group, Billard, posing like Rufus for their Rufisized album, 1975

Erings: (smiling) Uh, huh. You certainly did know how to work a pose, Beverley.

Beverley: Thanks, Erings. Years later, I realized that Rick James and I shared the same birthday, February 1st. It seemed ironic to me. I actually got the idea to write this book on the day I heard he had died. It was August 6, 2004, and it was reported that he had died of natural causes, in his sleep. Later, the cause was changed to a heart attack. He was only fifty-six years old.

He had been rumored to be a drug user. Of course, I didn't know the fact that we were born the same day at the time we first met him. I often wonder—if I had—

whether it might have been an icebreaker at that first meeting. Would I have felt somehow less intimidated? Unfortunately, I'll never know.

I knew of very few people with February 1st as a birth date. I know that Lisa Marie Presley is also a February 1st baby. And Tommy Smothers. But that's it. I had secretly always wanted to be born on February 12th, the day Abraham Lincoln was born; but now, I love that my birthday hasn't got a lot of other people to share it with. At least not people who get announced on *Entertainment Tonight*. And the "1" energy is the number of the trailblazer, of those who forge their own path in life and inspire others to find their distinct individuality as well. So, now I trust I was born on the perfect day for me.

Anyway, the day Rick James died is officially the day this book was born. I envisioned it as me telling anecdotal stories about my life, including this one of jamming with Rick James. That is also the day the title *Confessions of a Middle-Aged Hippie* originated.

Erings: Yes, Beverley, you are definitely a trailblazer from what I understand about you so far. I do personally remember meeting Rick James back in the '70s and he definitely left that "I'm outrageous" impression! I didn't know he was a fellow Aquarian. Definitely talented, and gone too soon.

Beverley: Somehow his death struck me very hard. For some reason, I felt very sad about it, and it made me start to question my own mortality.

Erings: But, you have experienced your own brush with mortality more than a few times, considering the dramatic health issues you have faced. Why would this be different?

Beverley: True enough, I guess. But I always saw my situation through rose-colored glasses, which allowed me to continue seeing my life events the way I *wanted* to see them. So, I probably never saw the critical or dire nature of my situation the way others did, since they were on the outside observing my life from their point of view. It's interesting. We all, at times, get caught up in only being able to see things through our perspective and thinking that it is the only one.

I was honestly never as scared about my imminent death as others seemed to be. I have been told a lot of things by a lot of different doctors, things that I generally didn't buy into. My reaction was always to immediately look for something else that I could have some hopeful belief in. I have always travelled my own path in spite of what others might have had me do.

I do enormous amounts of research, as you already know. Then I ask lots of questions and ultimately trust my intuition to make my choice. I rarely have people who agree with the choices I make for myself. For example, if I would have listened to the GI specialist who told me, when I was twenty-eight, that I'd never be able to get pregnant, that I'd be on drugs the rest of my life and that I'd inevitably have to have surgery again, well, I probably would have thrown up my hands and just given up.

Erings: What did you do?

Beverley: I didn't give up or give in. I basically decided to walk away from the traditional medical profession and seek an alternative option. In 1977, there weren't many MDs practicing complementary modalities, but I found the one doctor who was doing both. I had to literally beg his assistant to give me an appointment. He was in such high demand that I really didn't have a chance other than my persistent and eventually persuasive pleading.

Erings: So, was that the start of your alternative path?

Beverley: Yes, I would say it was. That was the beginning of me venturing farther and farther into a totally new and unfamiliar territory for myself, the emerging field of complementary and alternative medicine. Gratefully it not only resonated with me, but it worked for me as well and I have never looked back!

Erings: And I must admit you have tried a lot of things. Some of the things I haven't even heard of.

Beverley: (laughing) Yes, that is quite an understatement. I perhaps wasn't too adventurous with other areas of my life; but when it came to my health, I was game for anything. If I heard about something new, I would want to be the guinea pig and try it. I have always been willing to use myself as one large experiment.

From primal scream to the relaxation response and psychic surgery to past life regression, I tried intravenous therapy, cell injections, reflexology, acupuncture, chiropractic and colon therapy. I even consulted with a medical astrologer, which obviously fascinated me considering my interest in astrology. When he asked me if I had experienced certain health issues that he saw indicated in my chart, I was amazed at how accurate he was. Because I had.

I was literally open to trying anything that might help me find a way back to good health. When people talked about rebounding back in the '70s, I drove across town to buy a rebounder. I tried yoga and tai chi. I had never been much for physical exercise and I see now this has been quite detrimental for my overall well-being. Every time I tried something, my resistance would lead to some kind of injury. In yoga, an overzealous instructor pushed me into a knee injury.

I took every supplement imaginable, while simultaneously integrating homeopathy, Bach flower remedies and enzymes into my life. I tried so many different food programs, just trying to find the magic combination. I was always game when it came to myself. Each choice contributed to me taking one more step forward, but for me there was never a magic bullet. It was never one thing. Even though I thought the solution was something "out there," of course the answers are always within you. My curiosity, and willingness to continue searching, was my way of trying to bring the outside in.

Erings: Wow. I'm tired just listening to all that. I do relate to the different food programs though. And now?

Beverley: For me, currently, my staple protocol includes acupuncture and massage therapy. Although these appear to work only on the physical level, they actually work on more than just the physical level. All my therapists work on more than just that most obvious level of our being. They are all doing energetic healing work. I'm still striving for balance on the physical level. I still do some supplements and work with an anthroposophic doctor to continue to strengthen myself on a holistic level, but I'm not nearly the voracious consumer of new things as I once was. Perhaps I've learned to be discerning.

Erings: In English please?

Beverley: Well, my intention is to continue integrating all levels of my being—emotional, physical and spiritual, a.k.a. mind, body and spirit. They are all equally important. A disconnect in one leads to the imbalances in the others.

Erings: Okay, that makes it much clearer. I really do get that. After this short break, we'll talk more about your most recent health decline and your almost unbelievable rebound. And Beverley, hope you are ready, because I have got to get you to tell us more about this Daryl Hall thing.

Beverley: (smiling) Yes, Erings. I'm ready.

Erings: Stay with us for our next segment.

Return From The Living Dead

Erings: We're back with the intriguing Beverley Golden. It occurred to me during the break that it's the ideal time to talk about your most recent health scare. From what I understand, this one was the most serious and longest lasting of them all.

Beverley: In hindsight, it was definitely the most serious, but when you're in the middle of it, you don't necessarily see the bigger picture. It somehow becomes more about survival.

Erings: That's an interesting perspective. Tell us more.

Beverley: I was approaching my fifty-first birthday and the year leading up to it had been horrific for me. My father had died suddenly, after walking up a flight of stairs, at the age of fifty-one—and somehow, in my consciousness I felt like I was carrying his burden on my shoulders and that I might follow in his footsteps. Walking up a steep flight of stairs would panic me. I had developed somewhat of an uncontrollable fear, or maybe it was paranoia, that my fate would match his. Thankfully, I did reach my fifty-first birthday, but in actuality my father had been only two weeks shy of his fifty-second, so I realized that I had almost a full year to go.

Erings: You knew this might be considered an irrational fear?

Beverley: Of course intellectually I knew that, but his death was probably the single worst thing I had ever experienced in my life. His dying so young, and me being the same age, was something I couldn't digest. I had no way of processing losing him and just wasn't able to handle it.

It is amazing what fear can do to you. I see now how it can set you up and keep you living continually in a stressful place. Fear can paralyze you and for me, this fear of something my father had experienced happening to me, I believe, set off a whole chain of physical symptoms that had me spiral downhill again.

Erings: We understand that conceptually, but how exactly was it playing out for you? Returning to a place where your health and well-being are in such constant jeopardy?

Beverley: Well, Erings, there I was, fifty-one—and in December of 2000, just a couple of months before that year is up, I got sick around the holidays. It appeared to be just the flu, with all the expected symptoms. However, the symptoms didn't go away. Things were getting worse and worse and no one seemed to have an answer as to how to stop the ongoing diarrhea, complete body weakness and sheer exhaustion. No one, once again, knew exactly what was wrong with me. Before I knew it, I had basically lost 30 to 40 pounds and continued to decline very quickly. I believe I tried everything possible.

Erings: Wow, that is dramatic! With all your resources, it's amazing no one had any concrete answers.

Beverley: I know. No one. Although I had lots of people to go to for help and of course had been through this kind of thing a number of times before, the symptoms didn't let up. This was truly quite different. As almost a last-ditch effort, made spontaneously but out of desperation, I decided to go to a clinic in Germany. I had heard about it from within the healing community I was a part of, and found out that it was on the cutting-edge as a treatment facility. They were combining conventional medicine with complementary protocols.

Erings: That's a long trip to make in the condition you say you were in.

Beverley: I know it sounds like an unlikely choice, but I knew in relation to health issues, things in general are very much more progressive in Germany. The only concern, other than the long overseas trip that no regular medical professional would ever have sanctioned, was that the food they offered would be totally different from my current diet. It seemed virtually impossible it would work for me.

Erings: How were you thinking you could make it work for you?

Beverley: I talked to the clinic several times and they assured me they would do the best they could on the food issue. I ate a high-protein, organic, animal-based diet and their belief strictly prohibited any animal products at all. It was part of their philosophy. They occasionally would bring in hens' eggs and raw milk dairy products. This was going to be an enormous challenge for me to face. Monumental, actually.

Call me crazy, but I still decided to go. I cannot even believe it now, but desperation, coupled with my rose-colored-glasses view of the world, can make for amazing choices. This trip would be grueling even for the healthiest of people. Within one week of hearing about the clinic in May 2001, I was on a flight to Germany.

Erings: Did anyone support you on this decision?

Beverley: Everyone around me was worried about me being able to survive this trip. I remember landing at the Frankfurt airport and feeling like I was in some massive underground maze or city. I was the only person from my flight who seemed to be collecting their baggage. Or maybe now that I think of it, it just took me that long to walk from the plane to the baggage collection area. I had to ask someone to help me because I was so weak, there was no way I could even get my own bag off the carousel.

I made it to my waiting transport; wheelchair and all was there for me. The cherubic older lady made me feel so safe. I finally breathed a sigh of relief. I really believed I was off to be healed, or at least I had landed on the right path.

Erings: But it didn't quite work out that way, did it?

Beverley: No, not anything like it. When I first got there, I was grateful I had chosen a private room, even though this was an expensive choice I had made as well. Every single thing added more cost to this healing journey. I'd borrowed a lot of money from the equity in my house, just to be able to even consider it. By this point, I could only trust it would be worth it. That was the naïve part of me looking for "the" one answer. It was in some ways for me my last chance, and at this time it appeared that I had run out of options.

When I had my first exam with the head doctor, I had to take off all my clothes for him to assess me. Amazing what clothes can hide. I remember gasping in horror as I glimpsed my body in the full-length mirror. I remember thinking, "What has happened to my body?" I was only 89 pounds and literally bones with some very sallow skin on those bones. I was a living, walking skeleton. I was somehow back to the same place I had been at age twelve, as a very sick pre-teen. I knew then that I had a very long way to go, to get back to health.

Erings: But you were optimistic?

Beverley: (smiling) Of course. Or again, extremely naïve. I am always naïvely optimistic. But, how did I go so far down so quickly, and would I really be able to "recover" in just three weeks? I had always desired to be thin, but even I could see that this was not the way to do it. I do love the quick fix, but I believe I only started the healing journey during this time in Germany.

Erings: Tell us about your experience.

Beverley: Overall, although it was tiring and intense, it was fascinating. The experience captured my curiosity and it seemed everything they were doing there interested me.

I had the opportunity to be introduced to many new healing modalities and I met so many lovely and loving people, both staff and other patients.

This clinic was supported by the German health care system, which paid for German citizens to go there for yearly "health days." Extremely progressive compared to the system I am used to. Why wait until you are sick, when health days can contribute to your staying healthy?

Still, nothing I tried there seemed to work. I lay on the floor of my room a lot and had to put my feet up, as I was extremely swollen and virtually had trouble moving. I spent a lot of time watching the incredible landscape of clouds that would float past my window.

For the three weeks I was there, I couldn't even walk up a flight of stairs. I was in critical shape. Test after test and all they knew was that it was a very complicated set of intertwined issues. It seemed every internal organ was involved. One morning, one of my dear and favorite doctors came in and said that some of my blood tests were very troubling. All he could offer me was that I should begin to pray.

Erings: That does sound very serious. So you prayed?

Beverley: I did pray. I had people back at home praying, too. Everyone was expecting a miraculous recovery for me, or so I thought. I had actually heard a voice speak to me and say, "I am here for you. It is your time to heal." I held that in my consciousness even though when I told the doctors, they kindly told me that they did not believe that God speaks directly to individuals.

Erings: Care to share what you thought it was?

Beverley: I strongly believe that each of us are guided and supported by angels and other spiritual guides or helpers. They carry us through the good and bad times. I continuously asked for help and guidance and trusted that they were communicating to me, so I could feel supported in my unflappable belief that I would heal. It was certainly very real to me.

Erings: Lovely idea for us to envision. What are some of the strongest memories you brought back with you?

Beverley: Many, actually. One profound one is that I remember taking a bus ride into town with a group from the clinic to go to their place of worship. I could not even climb up the stairs to get on the bus. I was just physically too weak.

They were there to support and to help me, but I cried as we drove through the countryside and I saw all the people enjoying the spring weather, walking and bike riding. The staff at the clinic had warned me that I would probably *never* be able to travel again and told me that I must accept that my life would be extremely restricted from now on. This was very dramatic for me to hear.

Erings: I guess so. It seems doctors were always predicting your life for you, weren't they? Even if they weren't always correct.

Beverley: You've got that right, Erings. Now I am faced with this totally pessimistic, but to me unacceptable prognosis from even the alternative medical professionals—a prognosis that in many ways indicated I should not expect to recover.

These traditional medical doctors, who also worked in complimentary and alternative modalities, were giving me this news just before I was about to head home across the ocean again. The head doctor had seen limited possibilities for healing my physical body after examining me on arrival. However, as the days went on, they all saw my relentless inner fight and acknowledged that there might be more possibilities for healing than they originally predicted. But I'm still going home looking and being as unhealthy as I was when I got there. There was no noticeable change. There was no unnoticeable change either. Generally on a physical level there was absolutely no change at all.

Erings: Sounds like a devastating time for you.

Beverley: In many ways, it was. And then when I found out after the fact, long after, that my family—particularly my daughter—didn't even think I would come home alive, it was a shocking reality check. She had sent me off to Germany and kept saying that it was okay if I wanted to leave. Not understanding what she was saying, she had to elaborate that she was giving me permission to go to Germany and to die.

She was smiling at me on the outside at the airport when I left, but she was secretly saying goodbye to me, forever. She did not think I would return alive. In her eyes, she saw that I had gone downhill so quickly, tried so many things to get back to health and nothing seemed to be working this time. No definite diagnosis ever either. It wasn't so much that it was undiagnosable...it was just that it was highly complicated and had many components to what was happening in my physical body. It wasn't simply one thing that was wrong. That's how seriously ill I was.

Erings: That must have been very hard to hear from your daughter, Lani. Even my heart feels the sadness she must have been feeling.

Beverley: I know. It makes me sad when I think about it. (smiling) But, I did come back.

Erings: Did you ever think you might not?

Beverley: No, not that I consciously remember. When my daughter told me she was giving me permission to die, I remember being surprised and quickly reassuring her that I wasn't ready for that, not just yet. I told her that I still had a lot of things to do in this lifetime and not to worry. I would not be dying, just yet.

The gravity of my situation became very evident to me in Germany, but I had always found a way before. Always. This time (although I didn't know it then) was going to be a lot harder and take a lot longer than any previous experience. Many people continued to believe I was facing insurmountable odds. People back home thought it could go either way. I might live, but I might die.

I think the odds were more in favor of me dying. When I read the journals I wrote back then, I am reminded of how dire the entire situation was, yet all I see is my constant reaffirmation of hope and belief in what seemed to others to be impossible.

Erings: That's very admirable. I hope I would be as positive in the same situation.

So, now you are about to come home after three and a half weeks of constant therapy and support. Sorry, Beverley, but I think it would be good for people to have a visual of what you have been talking about. And I thank you in advance for letting us show this.

I heard a group gasp from the audience and as I looked out, saw many people covering their mouths and even their eyes. Mouths hung open in shock and disbelief. As I turned around and saw the picture, my heart sank and so many memories came flooding back.

Weighing in at 89 pounds on return from Germany in May 2001

This was the one picture I'd taken when I first arrived home, in just undies and a tank top, to chronicle what I looked like. On some maybe unconscious level, I knew that when I got better, this picture would be a reminder of where I'd had come from and to. Posing, like a muscle-bound body builder, with arms flexed to demonstrate biceps. No biceps in reality. No body in reality. Smiling, still smiling.

Beverley: Yes, Erings. When I see the picture I sometimes find it hard to believe I did make it back from there. And I do think it is important to see how critical I was. Pictures definitely do speak a thousand words. In my case, maybe more.

Erings: Beverley, that doesn't even look like you. Amazing to see the before and now. What happened then?

Beverley: The big question. What happened then.

I came home to the two-story house I live in. The only way up is thirteen very long stairs. Remember, Erings, I hadn't walked up a flight of stairs in three and a half weeks. Walking up those stairs was impossible for me to do at home now. I was hysterical the first few days. I'd been used to elevators and people always available to help me.

I had to get my mother to come over and help me. At eighty-five, that was really, really tough for her. Not only physically, but emotionally too. To have to watch your child be so sick and really not understanding why or how you can help. I think she thought I'd come home from Germany and be better. As she would say, "like the old Beverley," whoever that was in her mind.

Beverley, Lani and Lil, 1999 (just before my fall from health)

Erings: You talk about your mother as being a beacon of strength.

Beverley: Yes, she's someone people really like and admire. She's stubborn and opinionated, but that's her strength. It is what keeps her going. She's always been a great shoulder to cry on. Nothing affects her emotionally. Except when it has to do with her family, of course.

Erings: So now you are at home. What's next?

Beverley: Yes. Another million-dollar question. I was still sick and my dog, Stinky, had also been very sick. His health had been up and down. He was a seventeen-year-old Lhasa Apso and I was told by a friend that he wouldn't agree to go, until he knew that I was going to get better. We had a karmic bond and I needed to now give him permission to die.

I could hardly look after myself, so his health became an extra burden for me as well. No matter how sick he got, I refused to give up on him. People told me I was being cruel and should put him down, but I refused and kept looking for something else to give him a chance to get better. I tried all kinds of protocols and he would rally for a brief time and then decline. In some ways, he might have been mimicking me.

Erings: So interesting how our pets are both dependent on and interconnected to us. What did you do next?

Beverley: I turned to a nutritionist that I had worked with before I began to go downhill. The irony is that she lived downtown in a second-story walkup. The stairs were, to me, like climbing the steepest and tallest of mountains ever imaginable. She had even more stairs to climb at her place than I did at my house. She wanted me to come to her place two times a week for cell injections, which would not be possible for me to administer on my own. These injections had the potential to help with the rejuvenation process.

Erings: Insurmountable odds again?

Beverley: At first I was incredibly resistant to even taking that on. I did agree and frankly I have no idea how, but I mustered the small amount of strength I had and was determined to do it. Just driving downtown was nearly impossible. But the injections had to be put into the derrière, which I couldn't do myself, as I literally had no flesh to put the needles into. It was a torturous process.

We laughed about this recently, but at the time it was sheer will that kept me going. And, that is what she had told me. When she first saw me, after I returned from Germany, all that she could see was the light of determination in my eyes. That's what made her believe my recovery would be possible. That was it. It was the will to literally come back from the dead.

I continued to work with her for the next several months. In fact on Wednesday September 19, 2001, I had finally made an appointment for three o'clock in the afternoon to have Stinky, my dog, put down. It was unbearable to watch him be so sick. Similar to how it must have been for people to see how sick I was.

On that day, I travelled downtown to see her for my injection and as I was leaving, I called my daughter to say I was on my way home and to see how Stinky was. She told me she had taken him outside for some fresh air and laid him on the grass, so she could clean up his blanket. When she went out to get him, she found that he had just surrendered and died. I was stunned and in shock.

Again, I don't know if this was the best or the worst thing. For me, it was divine timing and took away any of the potential guilt I might have had for taking his life, even though he was unimaginably sick. For me also, I trusted that maybe he had seen something in me that told him I would get better. I'd continued to promise him that I would.

Several days after he died, I saw him—full of energy and life—and he was running toward the light. He stopped, turned his head and looked back at me to see if I was okay. He was checking to get my approval to move into the light. Tears flowed. I asked him to forgive me if I had not treated him well during my illness. Hopefully, he granted me that forgiveness as he turned around and ran into the light.

A picture of Stinky when he was in full health flashes up on the screen behind them and the audience sighs a big "ahh," like we do when we see a baby or animal that touches our hearts. Beverley can see some audience members wiping tears away from their eyes and everyone takes a moment to catch their breath.

Our beautiful-spirited Lhasa Apso, Stinky

Erings: Thanks so much for that, Beverley. Your story is powerful and very touching. It is interesting how we are called on to make choices for other living creatures. I adore dogs, so I know how tough that must have been for you. But you did continue on and fulfill your promise to Stinky: you did get better.

Beverley: I didn't appear to have any other acceptable option. For a very long time, I could not get above 96 pounds, no matter what I tried. To complicate the original prognosis of never being able to travel again, three weeks after I got back from Germany, I received a letter telling me that a blood test I had (before I had left Germany) had just come back indicating I had a very serious and potentially life-threatening liver disease.

This was another major setback, because it sent me into shock. No one here had ever even thought to test my liver. The specialist I had now been referred to here told me that, unless I did major drug therapy, I would absolutely need a transplant. No options on this one. This seemed almost too much to bear. Maybe some cruel joke on me.

Erings: So you chose to do the drugs?

Beverley: No, not even close. What I did do, was an enormous amount of healing work around this issue, calling on every alternative therapy and protocol I could find. From homeopathic remedies to art therapy, and many things in between, I worked with the emotional and spiritual levels of all my physical issues.

On my last visit to this same specialist, he actually told me that maybe I didn't need to see him anymore. He was visibly shocked and continued to check back through all the records he had for me, as if to confirm that he had been correct in his diagnosis.

However, he admitted that I was doing so well that my family doctor could monitor me now. So, I went from the prognosis of needing a transplant, to him telling me he didn't need to see me anymore.

Erings: That's incredible. From transplant to all clear.

Beverley: Basically. I trusted my own judgment, did an enormous amount of research and did the necessary healing work over a period of many, many years. There was no magic pill or quick fix for me. I'd like to believe that the results speak for themselves, though!

In fact, I might add that it is extremely important to listen to how you are feeling as opposed to what the outside tests might tell you. There have been so many times when I was feeling good and yet as soon as tests came back with troubling results, I would spiral downhill, becoming overly focused on those results, as opposed to how I was actually feeling.

Conversely, there were times when I wasn't feeling well, believing something was wrong, but the tests didn't set off any alarm bells. That didn't necessarily make things better either—so I say that you must really pay attention to how YOU are feeling, not how someone or something else, like a test, tells you you are feeling. Again, trusting your own judgment is the key. It isn't something you can teach really, but it is something you can practice.

Erings: Sounds like it. Amazing what personal choice based on intuition can yield. Let's continue. What happened next? You are having the cell injections, and?

Beverley: Somehow, I was divinely led to a woman who did classical homeopathy and really wanted to help me. I was at her house one day for a consultation, and she pulled out a painting to show me.

It was a veil painting, a style of painting used in a local art school and based on anthroposophy. It intrigued me. She smiled and said that she thought I would like it. This, I believe was a major turning point for me. I was very drawn to this painting style and she suggested I consider taking some classes with the director of an art school called Arscura. I was still too sick to even consider embarking on even a weekend program; but like so many other things with me, once I am struck by something and it stays with me, I will eventually find my way to it.

Erings: Sounds like you were committed and determined, regardless of how long it took.

Beverley: (smiling) Yes, life definitely continues to give me opportunities to practice patience, Erings.

Very slowly but surely, I did gain some strength. I was still painfully skinny. I even remember one of the first times I went out to a restaurant after coming home from Germany, bringing my own cushion to sit on, as chairs were too uncomfortable for my scrawny, bony derrière.

On my way to the washroom, I passed a table with two young guys involved in a heated conversation. One of them looked up at me and actually said, "God bless you." I thanked him, but was very thrown by that. What did he mean? Did I actually look that scary? In fact, I did. I looked frighteningly close to death as you just saw.

Erings: Yes, Beverley, we just saw how close to death you looked in that picture. But that piece of art stayed with you.

Beverley: It really did. As if it spoke directly to me. I did eventually begin to take weekend workshops with Regine through Arscura. I absolutely was intrigued by this veil painting. I decided to enter the full-time Art For Life program. I sincerely believe that Regine is one of those Earth angels who help people facilitate their own healing. I felt enormously blessed to have her come into my life. She also suggested I see one of the anthroposophic doctors, who would be another of the divine things sent to me in my life.

I began to see a massage therapist, who remains one of the key players in my support team. She has become much more than that as well, a friend and an objective advisor or witness who helps me to see a clear perspective. She is one of the people who told me that when she first saw me walking into her clinic, her initial thought was, "This could go either way." Outer appearances are deceiving and once she started to get to know me, she was shocked to see how active and alive I continued to be.

Erings: How long did all of this continue for you?

Beverley: For three years, I would go one day each week for the Art for Life program. It was grueling and at times nearly impossible for me. I wasn't sure how I would do it. Sometimes I would have to lie on the floor to even make it through a class. I was, however, committed. I believe that commitment is crucial in being successful at whatever you try.

The work that Arscura does is truly quite amazing. Because you are entering into a soul process, you have the opportunity to heal on a very deep level. No physical healing can happen without some soul healing, too. I now understand that physical illness manifests where there is a disconnect from your soul. Maybe that sounds esoteric to some, but I invite others to ask themselves how it is possible if we are physical, emotional and spiritual beings, that an illness would only happen on the physical level.

Erings: For those who do believe we are multidimensional beings, of course that would make sense. How would you describe how Arscura helped you?

Beverley: For me, a person who always wants to go from A to Z as fast as possible, this process work became a key for me in learning a new way to be in the world. I believe it helped to save my life. After I finished the Art for Life program, I entered another three-year program called Biography – Life As Art. This work has continued to uplift and inspire me to make my own changes. I believe our souls speak through colors, so the art, especially the painting, was incredibly therapeutic and healing.

It was always challenging for me to stay in the program. At the time, the people I was working for didn't even know that I was doing the courses.

Erings: You were working?

Beverley: I was. Still trying to do it all. My employers were very kind and treated me like part of the family. I was working in the food industry, and I worked away from the office most of the time. They trusted me to do my own thing and as always, I made the situation work for me.

Slowly and surely, I started to make progress. I gained more and more strength but didn't gain weight. I would eat massive quantities of food—sometimes even 4,000-plus calories a day—but still I did not gain weight. And no, I was not engaged in serious exercise to account for the calories. The truth is I was so sick, I barely exercised at all.

Erings: What??

Beverley: I know it sounds impossible, but my body was totally malabsorbing most of what I was eating. In fact, my doctor believed that if I was going to die of anything, it would be from malnutrition, not any specific organ disease.

Erings: So obviously something dramatic happened, because you are looking healthy and normal to us all now.

Beverley: Yes, thank you. I guess that is true. It was a long seven years of one step forward and two steps back. To continue on, in early 2008 it was suggested by my current GI specialist (whom I saw when I needed iron infusions) to just go and see a surgeon, because my bowel appeared to be getting worse, with severe strictures in multiple places. I asked her who she was recommending these days. When she mentioned the same surgeon who had done my surgery in 1986, I immediately agreed.

Erings: Any particular reasons you agreed this time?

Beverley: Well, Dr. C. was now head of surgery and was *the* surgeon you would want, if you did want surgery. I was willing to appease all the doctors who wanted me to explore all options. In my own mind though, if I am totally honest, I really had no intention of even considering surgery!

Along with malnutrition, I was chronically anemic and nothing ever helped me overcome this. As I mentioned, I had repeated iron infusions, a process where they infuse a large dose of iron intravenously. I'd also had intramuscular injections week after week, which leave your derrière tattooed black, but none of that ever helped me for very long. I had two-toned buttocks, but my blood was not any better.

Jump to a beautiful, breezy June day. I meet with Dr. C. and what he told me was mind-blowing. I had hoped he might say that he could improve the quality of my life by 60 to 70 percent. I wondered if even that would be enough to have me sincerely consider surgery. But forget the 60 to 70 percent. He said that he could guarantee, with 90-percent certainty, that having surgery would improve my overall well-being. Ninety percent! I left and started crying, because now the odds were stacking in the opposite direction—but only if I chose to have the surgery. How could I resist the odds? I was to go away, think about it and let them know. They couldn't do it until September anyways. I know most people are probably wondering why I'd even hesitate.

Erings: (smiling) Yes, Beverley, we are.

Beverley: Well, for me it was a huge dilemma. What to do? I had vowed never to go under the knife again. I would never let my gut be cut open. Three times was more than enough.

I'd also say that, for many of us, we have a lot invested in a certain identity we have created for ourselves. It could be: "I'm always the strong one for everybody, I can't show my emotions." Or for me, it was an ongoing question I asked myself: "Who are you without this illness?" Yes, who am I? Back to that personal identity and self-worth issue.

Most of my life was lived as a person who has health issues. What would it be like to now be someone without illness as my story? I really had no point of reference, so I see that subconsciously and consciously, that was a very alive question for me.

Erings: That is a very profound point you are making, Beverley. I would imagine we all have an identity that we have come to believe is who we are. What made you go forward even with awareness of this?

Beverley: I chose to go in to see the surgeon prepared with lots of questions. I had listed all my no's, which he somewhat surprisingly, I admit, agreed to support me on. No drugs. Okay. No nasogastric tube. Okay. And I had lots of other questions and all his answers sounded too good to be true. So in a way, it was virtually impossible to say no. (smiling) Even I am not that stubborn or that naïve.

Erings: Nice to hear that, Beverley.

Beverley: Thanks. All my life I had tried to prove I was right, sometimes at the expense of my health. Sometimes that "proving them wrong" attitude worked for me, and I would prove I was right and they weren't. This time I had to switch that thinking around. I think I also finally realized that my health was more important than proving I was right. There is a spiritual question that asks, "Would you rather be right or happy?" Right had always seemed so important to me up until now. Now I understand that there is no right and no wrong. Just a point of view or perspective.

Erings: That is very insightful. But, what did proving you were right have to do with this situation?

Beverley: Well, I'd been trying to avoid surgery to prove I could heal on my own terms, making my own choices. I was constantly fighting for my way to be the *only* way. This doctor was willing to allow me lots of leeway. Starting with the healing people I wanted to come in after the surgery, he was willing to be open and considerate of all the things that were important to me. Genuinely open. He was meeting me halfway, or farther, in a lot of respects.

Somehow I was able to see that maybe it wasn't just my way, or their way. I went away from this meeting and talked about it to a lot of people. The response was universally the same. Ninety percent!! How can you refuse those odds, Beverley?

I even had a dream that I was having dinner with him and his wife, who referred to him as not only a surgeon, but an artist. A surgical artist. That dream felt very powerful to me. I really resonated with that image. I would become one of his surgical works of art.

Erings: Did you have a moment when you knew you had absolutely made the right choice to go ahead?

Beverley: Interestingly, there were two moments. The first one was when I called the surgeon's office to ask when the soonest he could do the surgery would be, and was told that they had already tentatively booked me in for September 16, 2008. I was very taken back by this. Was this a good omen? It felt right. Astrologically it checked out.

So I was going to have surgery on September 16th. I had several repeat meetings with the surgeon to ask all my myriad of additional questions, and things kept looking more and more in my favor. However, trust faded a bit just before my last pre-surgery meeting with the surgeon. I still had a few more questions to ask. As I'm driving downtown envisioning the perfect parking spot, of course, there it is waiting for me just outside the hospital. Perfect.

Then I get out of the car to put money in the meter and I see a once beautiful, dead bird, guts all over the place. I had a moment of panic. Maybe this was an omen, too. I was very struck by this and couldn't get it out of my mind.

Erings: It fascinates me how affected you are by the signs you receive. But, you still go ahead.

Beverley: I do. But that image remained a constant reminder of my fears.

However, the second positive sign came the morning that I checked into the hospital. It was actually 6:00 a.m. on the day of my surgery and I had been praying for a private room. I'd been told that the chances of a private room were almost nil, as they had closed the wing that housed those rooms. It felt very important to me and since I was willing to pay, I really wanted my own space. When I found out that I would get a private room, I knew I had made the right decision.

I was smiling from ear to ear, even though in a few hours I would be having major abdominal surgery and smiles would be hard to come by. In fact, I was to be the first person this private room was opened up to since the wing had been shut down. This certainly seemed like a positively good omen to me.

I proceeded to decorate the room, now my room, with flowers and my artwork to create an uplifting, safe and joyful space to recover in. I created an energy in this room that somehow drew people to it. My surgeon admired the amethyst crystal I'd brought in. No words were spoken, but I took it as his way of somehow acknowledging that maybe what I believed in did have some positive impact.

Erings: That sounds very affirming for a person like you.

Beverley: It was. Because I truly believe that life isn't only about science and statistics. It is about humanity, belief and energy. Something much grander than merely the sensory world we are so caught up in. The nurses enjoyed coming into my room, because in many ways I was told I was not the typical patient. That wasn't too surprising to me, obviously. The doctors were universally surprised at how quickly I healed, how little pain medication I needed and how quickly I was up and mobile.

I had my Reiki therapist come in daily for four-hour treatments. She is another one of the people who has witnessed my downs and has always believed in the possibility that I would regain my state of health. Of course I had my own food—homemade organic jello and soup. All of these things together made a huge difference.

Erings: So, there was no doubt from that moment of checking in?

Beverley: Well, there was one moment of sheer and absolute panic-filled doubt. It was the morning of the surgery as well. All the patients and their families were sitting on chairs outside the surgical room. Just waiting. It was the protocol for the surgeon to come and greet his patient and for the anesthetist to come and give his reassurances, too. In my case, this is where it all could have fallen apart very easily.

In the pre-surgery prep meeting, I had met with the "Deepak Chopra" of anesthetists and although he warned me that I might not get him on the actual day of the surgery, he assured me he would recommend a highly specific protocol for me. It was designed to cut down on the drugs, but still offer effective pain relief. He advised me that he was going to suggest a new procedure that not all anesthetists would be willing to use.

So, I just assumed that it was divined that I would get him. But, instead of Chopra, I get Wild Bill Hickok. He is talking and smiling at me, my daughter and my mother in a somewhat cocky way and saying to trust him because "that's why they pay him the big bucks." I'm now looking for the closest available exit and wonder how fast I can run away in hospital slippers and gown. That running scene is just in my mind, and of course I don't actually run. My mother and daughter are voicing their own concerns about him, too.

Erings: Interesting how one small comment like that can unnerve you.

Beverley: Well, Erings, it didn't end there. In the operating room, he is somewhat frustratedly attempting to start an IV in my left arm, which I assure him has no viable veins. Years of experience tell me I'm right, and in this case he is not going to be successful. He continues to try and finally reluctantly moves to my right arm, which he mutters will get in the way of the surgeon, and proceeds to keep uttering stuff about how emaciated I am.

He asks what I've been eating and when I tell him a high-quality organic diet, he suggests that maybe I should change what I'm eating. He now blows any possible veins in either arm and says he has to go in my neck to start the IV. I am protesting very loudly. I'm not going to go down without a fight! Right then, he announces that they are going to now put in a breathing tube. I immediately know that this means my nose and/or throat are going to be involved. I loudly protest, *"I Don't Do Tubes."* He says something like, "They pay me the even bigger bucks to make sure you wake up, so yes, you do."

Erings: Sounds like quite an interesting way to start a surgery.

Beverley: Interesting, but in a rather unusual way, Erings. Here I was, planning to have some wild and memorable soul journey during surgery, convinced I would astral travel and meet up with other wandering souls, returning with stories that would fascinate and captivate people. However, instead, I woke up in the recovery room with lots of other people who hadn't woken up yet. His last words were the only thing I remembered. At least he had been good to his word...I had woken up.

Beside me in the recovery room was a woman who apparently wasn't breathing and who wouldn't wake up. This appeared to not be a great situation for her. Several nurses were screaming her name very loudly, hoping that she would remember who she is, start breathing and come to.

When I asked about my pain protocol (just to make sure), the nurse told me that the anesthetist had vetoed it. I was noticeably upset, which is *not* a good thing to be after having your abdomen cut open.

Erings: Not really, but his part in the surgery is now totally over. Right?

Beverley: Not exactly. As they wheeled me back to my room, the anesthetist was coincidentally in the same elevator. After I blurted out my desire for "Chopra's" pain protocol, he replied, "You're too emaciated for that!" And then, as an aside, he said, "Oh yes, and you'll have a small scar on your right arm, because I couldn't get the IV started. We've steri-stripped it and hopefully the scar won't be too bad." I looked at him, in a post surgery daze, and said, "You're a rascal!" He questioned, "A rascal?" And *that* was it. He got off the elevator and became my one broken link in the whole process.

Erings: I must admit, it is kind of a funny story in the midst of this serious experience. I am constantly surprised at how you will fight for your belief with all you've got. And considering how well you say you did, you must have been very prepared.

Beverley: Yes, always be prepared. Isn't that the Scouts' motto or something? But for me, in all aspects of life, you do your homework, ask the questions, use your intuition and make your decision. Wow, sounds like I am a Scout.

But, seriously, the nurses and doctors and residents were so amazed with my recovery that I was dubbed the Golden Girl, both literally and figuratively. In some ways, being prepared is what I've always done; but it has become clearer and clearer to me, as I get older, exactly how to do it. Hopefully, I'm getting wiser, or my level of understanding is deepening. Whatever it is, I believe that individuals must take responsibility for themselves. Don't always depend only on other people or what they tell you. Regardless of if they are doctors, loved ones or whatever role they may play in your life. Only you can decide what is ultimately the best thing for your highest good.

Erings: Very well said. It's so true that many people don't really listen to their inner voice. I guess fear plays a big part. As you know, I always say, "This is what I'm certain of." At some point you have to be certain of some things in your life. So, to all of you listening out there: take responsibility for yourself! I'm sure our listeners would be interested in hearing what they actually did do in this surgery.

Beverley: Well, the surgeon had to remove one more foot of my jejunum, the first part of the small bowel. It was horribly disfigured, swollen in places and severely narrowed in others. I'd already had two feet out during the surgery when I was fourteen, so now I had a total of three feet gone. One of the main things I wanted was for the three metal clips that had lived in my bowel since my very first surgery, to be removed. And from what the surgeon told me, he believed it had to be in the section he removed, because everything else looked perfect and normal. This is one time that normal was a very good thing.

Erings: But there is one very specific request you made.

Beverley: I did. I asked if they could get the specimen from pathology, because I wanted to see it. That certainly created quite a stir. They didn't understand why I would want to see it and of course they said I was the first patient who had *ever* made such a request. Every day I'd ask and explain I wanted to see this small part of my body that was creating such havoc. To have an opportunity to say goodbye to it and acknowledge that it was finally gone.

I even stayed an extra night, as they promised me for sure they would be able to bring it up to me. On the morning I'm about to leave, the last-minute news is that they cannot possibly let it leave the lab, but they will take a color picture of it and forward it to the surgeon.

Erings: You really pushed to see this piece of bowel that they removed?

Beverley: I did. And true to their word, I did get a full color picture to amaze and wow all who care to look at it.

Erings: Well, you've had the surgery, you are the Golden Girl. Now what. What happens next?

Beverley: I am given a specific diet I must follow for four weeks and am instructed not to lift anything heavy for six weeks. Seems pretty doable. I go home and begin to eat. That's always the easy part for me. Pretty much like I did before. Lots of food, large quantities. I didn't gain weight before, so why would I *possibly* think I will now? Am I ever in for a very rude awakening!

Within a short time, I began to gain weight and by the end of ten weeks, I had gained 30 pounds. I felt like I was on a runaway train to the exact place I never wanted to go again: being of sizable weight. Let me off this train! Although I did need to gain *some* weight, I was way past that point by now. At one point I had trouble walking and I swear my feet were screaming up at me, "What the hell are you doing up there?"

The adjustment was completely unexpected and very difficult. My hair was falling out from the anesthesia. Him again! Couldn't shake that rascal. No one had prepared me for any of these after-surgery possibilities. However, in looking back at the 1986 surgery, I had also gained a lot of weight very quickly. But I thought it was because of the crazy drugs I'd been convinced I needed.

Erings: Thirty pounds is a lot of weight to gain that quickly! How are you dealing with it now?

Beverley: In many ways, this is a lifelong issue for me. The only time I've ever been at the weight where I think I look good is when I've been sick.

Erings: Wow. That is quite a heavy burden you carry in a desire to be thin.

Beverley: It is. It seems the only way I've been able to experience my body is when there is pain, and the only time there is pain is when I'm sick. And yet, that is the only time I can be the weight I want to be. It's like I have the appearance of someone with an eating disorder, yet I don't have one. I have thought many times that I have an eating *pattern* disorder. That to me is different.

I have this unhealthy love affair with food. I do adore food. My happiest time, especially when my daughter and I go on vacation, is after we've gone to the local health food store. The stuff we buy, the stuff we try. Hmmm. As it is well known, food always represents something other than just food. It is emotional comfort for many of us.

Erings: I do know that for sure. So are you a good cook, considering you choose to make most of your own meals?

Beverley: Well, yes, but not in the way you are asking. I like simple ingredients, mostly fresh, with really little preparation and no muss and fuss. I love eating, not so much the cooking.

Erings: Yeah. I hear you on that one. I love eating too, as you all know. I've had my own issues with food. I still can't get over that you used to eat 4,000 calories a day, without any exercise, and didn't gain weight!

Beverley: Well, I certainly relate more to that now, than to how I was before. But on many levels, I understand it more now. I have now settled into a comfortable body weight and trust I am in a healthy place, not expecting those swings up and down ever again.

Erings: It sounds like you've reached a place of some acceptance, maybe even some peace with it all.

Beverley: Thanks, Erings, I believe so. Women really do have a harder time with this than men do, don't we? I often wonder if men really care as much as women do. In our society, it is the focus for females. The elusive "perfect" physical image. For women, we strive for beauty. Men strive for power.

Erings: So, now you are healthy and obviously your life has changed.

Beverley: Dramatically. In fact, I am in a diametrically opposed place to where I was in 2001. I realize that I have spent more of my life unhealthy than healthy. Now that I am healthy, that eight or nine years of such desperately poor health is like a surreal part of my story that is really hard to connect with. It is interesting that so many people who first met me then (when I was sick) are amazed at how healthy I am now. In some ways, I have resurrected myself and I do not usually give myself too much credit for that.

Erings: Why do you think that is?

Beverley: I think because I have done it so many times before. It feels like it is just one more time to me. I admit it was much harder and the road to recovery was a very steep climb. I don't want to do it again, though. I believe I have paid my dues and that is some past part of what I needed to do to become who I am from here forward.

As I always say to people, all things are possible. Do not give up. Be informed. Get informed. Speak up and out for yourself. I get frustrated with people who give up without really trying. I'm not here to judge, but I often wonder how many people might have saved themselves by stepping up and taking charge. In a way, it is the same as the people who when asked how things are say, "Oh, you know. Same old, same old." How do you settle for that? For me, the joy in life is that every day is a new day filled with possibilities. We can't even imagine the magnitude of what our lives can be. I never would have imagined during those desperately sick years that it would be possible to be where I am right now.

Erings: You would be a great patient advocate.

Beverley: Thanks, Erings, I have been told that. A person has to want to have someone else speak out and up for them. I am working on a new book that will be called *How To Survive Being a Patient,* as I have in many ways been a patient since I was twelve years old.

I am a very vocal consumer advocate, too. If you don't speak up, no one will know what you are thinking or how you are feeling. I think it is important to point out the positive as well as the negative. I encourage people to speak up. To ask questions. Change a life, maybe one small deed at a time.

Erings: I like to live my life that way, too. I do believe we all have a responsibility, not only to ourselves, but to others as well. Let's take a much-needed break. When we come back, we'll talk about how you actually came about writing your book, after sitting with the seed of the idea for nearly a decade.

You Too Can Write a Book in Eight Days

Erings: You talk about the seed of this book coming to you the day you heard the news that Rick James died. What led you to actually write the book?

Beverley: I had been experiencing a bout of debilitating high fevers during the spring and summer of 2004. Once again, there was no obvious explanation. I would be in a delirium and these crazy memories would come flooding back. One day, I was lying on the floor with cold compresses on my head. Ideas were exploding. I was talking crazy words, or so my daughter says. The day Rick James died, I actually sat down and started to write what I thought might be individual chapters. It was me recalling old memories and putting them down as self-contained stories. I wrote eight or so and jotted down other ideas over the course of the next few years.

Erings: Like the mynah bird and the rabbi story? I honestly still can't get over that one.

Beverley: Well, yes. I had this idea that it could be a magazine column or a weekly newspaper column, but I never found the motivation to finish it. Nowadays it could have even been a blog. I'm never at a shortage for real-life stuff to talk about.

Erings: So what happened next?

Beverley: Well, then, after not traveling for two years, I went back to Sedona, Arizona, in the summer of 2009.

Erings: Being that Sedona is known for its high spiritual vibration, I can't wait to hear what happened for you there!

Beverley: Sedona certainly is a highly spiritual place, making it a great place to create new possibilities. What happened, on the surface, was one of those seemingly innocent conversations on a hot summer day in a swimming pool. I was talking to this woman about art and Arscura. She told me she was an artist and a writer and had been for many years.

From out of nowhere, she tells me she just had a fascinating experience at a writing retreat in the area: You literally write a book in eight days. I'm sure you know enough about me by now to know that as soon as I heard a book could be written in eight days, I was beyond excited!

Although she had actually been a writer for twenty-five years, she admitted this process was quite different for her and she would consider doing it again. She confirmed that everyone wrote a book during the retreat. No exceptions in her group. I asked about coming in with preconceived ideas and about not wanting to work on a computer. She answered all my questions and told me the man who devised this method had been teaching it successfully for twenty-five years. You attend . . . you write a book in eight days.

Erings: Okay. That seems like an impossible task.

Beverley: I initially thought that, too, but of course the "I'm-not-a-process-person, the-shorter-the-better" part of me came screaming to the surface. She promised to contact me with the information I needed, but I never heard from her again.

I came back home and couldn't stop telling people about it, even though all I knew was what some stranger had told me at the pool. I was so drawn to it. It stayed with me and I couldn't shake it. I was having an ongoing dialogue with myself about the fact that I needed to do this. I needed to finally, once and for all, see if I was a writer. I did some research and it was very easy to find exactly what I needed to know. Good marketing will do that for you. I was continuously thinking about it and knew, for whatever reason, I must step in and do it.

Erings: Don't you love those moments of synchronicity?

Beverley: I absolutely do. Sometimes I think my life has been divinely guided like that. I was aware that I couldn't attend the next retreat in October of '09. The next one after that would be in March 2010. I believe I was the first person to sign up in late October or early November, just after the October retreat had ended. I'd made my commitment and now I'd have to wait again for what turned out to be four torturous months for me.

Erings: That appears to be a theme for you, too. Make a decision and then have to wait for the event to arrive.

Beverley: Yes, a lot of times I don't make a decision too easily—but when I jump, well, I really jump. I'm the hurdler or the broad jumper who really goes for it and is in it to win it. It's an interesting analogy because I am honestly the least athletic person in maybe the whole world. I used to get my mother to write notes so I could be excused from gym class, especially when any kind of equipment was involved. Balance beams or even floor mats threw me into a panic. I was, to put it mildly, a first-class spazz. I was the kid who couldn't catch a ball because I was blinking my eyes so much I couldn't see it. Or else I would have my hands in front of my eyes.

Our only family sport was skating. My dad was not at all athletic; he skated on his ankles. Although I could skate, I fell a lot. My mother, on the other hand, had been an all-star athlete as a young girl. Speed skater, competitive swimmer, volleyball team captain and all-star baseball player. In a way, I think being athletic from a young age saves one later in life.

When my mother was young, it was the customary source of activity. There were no televisions or radios and kids just went to the park and played. Physical activity was part of their life back then. We know now that being physically active contributes to our overall well-being, so I would imagine that my mother, being so athletic when she was young, could only have contributed to her health and longevity.

Erings: (laughing) That's *not* good news for me.

Beverley: (smiling) Back to the writing retreat. I had so much time to prepare—mentally and physically. I worked with an osteopath for two months to help build up my core and postural muscles to support my arm and shoulder. I planned to write longhand, because that is the best way to access a deeper part of yourself and write from the heart.

I also purchased a new MacBook, which presented a whole new challenge and plunged me into a steep learning curve. I simultaneously started a couple of other regimens too, including faithfully walking each day and changing up my diet, plus reading about the art of writing. Somehow I arrived at a place of information overload. I experienced difficulty sleeping, as my mind was racing all the time.

Then, once I started the pre-retreat protocol of listening to the subliminal CDs, the book literally began pouring out line-by-line in my mind. We weren't to write anything down, so I would walk for thirty minutes a day—that was new for me, too—listening to the subliminal "transitioning back to the writer within" CD and having an inner-mind dialogue that began to appear to be a book.

Erings: What was coming up for you?

Beverley: It was partly these memories, which I'd already started writing down years before, and partly spiritual learnings, or pieces of wisdom I'd assimilated, for lack of a better description. The words wouldn't stop. I was in many ways writing a book without putting any pen to paper. When I got to the retreat, I literally couldn't stop my brain. Often the book you think you are going to write isn't the one that comes out. I guess this was the book for me to write first, because it poured out effortlessly.

It is really powerful to remove all distractions and get into a zone where you are writing six-plus hours a day, with other people who are there to do the same thing. Also synchronistically, I met three people at this retreat who continue to be friends to this day.

Erings: Those connections must have made the experience so much richer for sure. You also mentioned that the four-month wait brought up lots of doubts and questions.

Beverley: Yes, Erings. With a racing mind and lack of sleep, I was becoming very hyper and for whatever reason was doubting my decision. I asked the facilitator question after question, and at the retreat he asked me to be a participant on a retreat re-cap radio broadcast. He actually announced that I had set the record for the most questions *ever* asked before and during a retreat. I am known for asking lots of questions; I thought I was just making sure I was prepared. I even connected with a guy who attended the October retreat who had offered to help me. On one occasion, I just needed to email and ask, "How much does a finished book weigh?"

Erings: You *are* kidding?

Beverley: (smiling) Actually, no, I'm not. After all, I had baggage and weight restrictions. I thought if I'm writing loads and loads of pages in longhand, I might have a lot of notebooks to bring home. It does seem silly now, but I really needed to know. Shows you what happens when you think too much. I believe the term is *overthinking*. It's okay if people laugh at me as long as I'm laughing, too. He thought I was asking how much the ink would weigh down the pages.

Erings: So, Beverley, how much does a finished longhand book weigh?

Beverley: (smiling) Maybe 2-3 pounds.

Erings: Okaaay! So how many words *are* in these books?

Beverley: It varies by person. Maybe 50,000 words. Most people write at a pace of 1,500 to 2,400 words an hour. It sounds tiring, but it works. Believe it or not, my experience confirms that it isn't necessary to toil and labor for months or years. I went through it and basically birthed this book in those eight days. Not counting all the pre-retreat idea streaming that happened beforehand. I will also qualify that it was really only the germ of the book that was written during that time. It is quite impossible to have a totally finished and polished book in that short amount of time. It took lots of additional hours after to hone it and get it to the place where it was finished and ready to be born into the world.

Erings: That sounds more like it.

Beverley: There are authors who do spend hours, days and months creating their books, but I believe that is because they are working from a left-brain place. The left-brain makes it difficult to create the flow. It is the analytical side of the brain. The right brain is the creative and non-linear part. Writing doesn't have to be long and arduous at all. With the method I used, you connect to the creative right brain and let the book flow from the heart. The process is quite amazing and it works if you follow it.

Erings: What about research?

Beverley: The method asks you to do research *after* you have written the book. Generally, research comprises only 2 to 3 percent of the total content.

Erings: So does everyone really write a book at this retreat?

Beverley: I would say it makes a great starting point. Based on my experiences (I went back a second time to start another book), everyone is able to get into a creative right-brain space and produce at the very least the outline or beginnings of what will become a finished book. Of course, the after-retreat part requires the *real* work, as there is much more to the whole process than merely the book writing. I guess I found out that was the easy part.

Erings: Would you say *anyone* can write a book?

Beverley: There was a *New York Times* article that indicated 81 percent of people surveyed said they would love to write a book. Being someone who always wanted to see if I could write a book, this was an excuse to jump in and see what would emerge.

Erings: Fascinating! Eighty-one percent is a *huge* number, although I'm sure most people don't ever get around to actually writing one. I, for one, am glad you were led to the retreat and that you wrote this book. I'd say what you have shared in this book is so candid, we all can relate to your experiences as paralleling our own in many ways.

In our upcoming segment, we'll explore a lot of other fun stuff we've been waiting to hear about including: Beverley's life as a mom, her adventures as a spiritual seeker, and another synchronistic meeting with one of the sexiest pop stars of our time. Stay tuned! We'll be right back.

Take it to The Max

Erings: Beverley, I'm so intrigued by your meanderings, I barely know where to head next. Let's talk a bit about your daughter, Lani. You've said your life literally changed the day she was born. Your book articulates—quite insightfully, I might add—how so many of your experiences are intertwined with hers.

Beverley: Well, Erings, Lani *is* incredibly special. I know all mothers say that about their children, but I'm fortunate to have other people tell me that about her, too. She is loving, talented in so many ways, and sincerely delightful. She has a sweetness and the kind of personality that draws people in. Not in a conniving or manipulative way, but just because of who she is.

Sometimes it also works out that a mother and daughter have a relationship that becomes one of good friends as well. I believe that is why Lani and I can share so many experiences together. It always feels natural. Although she is diametrically opposed to me in her approach to life, we are both air signs. So in some ways, we have a lot in common. Air signs are the thinkers, the idea people who hopefully bring the ideas down to earth.

Lani and I both love theatre, especially musical theatre, so we enjoy a lot of that together. And, we laugh and laugh together. I make her laugh and we love the same humor in movies and television. Actually, Lani has had a fair amount of fame and notoriety since her youth. She was the co-star of her own television show from age eleven, for six-plus years. The show provided an amazing time and opportunity for her and then for us, too. We travelled to New York, L.A. and London, staying in wonderful hotels, all expenses paid, and from time to time rubbing shoulders with very well-known people.

Like mother, like daughter, circa 1995

Erings: Care to share some names?

Beverley: Sure. Isn't that part of the fun of this? One particular time, we were traveling to L.A. first class, after the Gemini Awards in Toronto, and basically the entire first-class section was made up of the four of us, Lani and me and her co-star and her mother, plus *Second City* alumni—Eugene Levy, Martin Short, and Catherine O'Hara were the three I remember. These people actually recognized my daughter and her co-star for their work in their show *Ready or Not*, and told them so. It was really a nice moment for the girls, and I must say for me, too.

Another time, Lani and I were in Disneyland, just standing in line for a ride like everyone else, and we heard a woman screaming, "Oh my God! It's you!" We looked around, not sure what we were expecting to see. And after a minute, we realized she was pointing at Lani. Lani was the "you" she was talking about. She was visiting from Mexico and said that she loved my daughter, would recognize her smile anywhere, and could she please take a picture with her?

Lani always obliged. I'm sure there are thousands of pictures of Lani with admiring fans out there in the world. These are just a couple of the memories we share.

Erings: Would you tell us more about *Ready or Not* for those who might not have seen it? I know about the show, and I also know it was hugely successful and syndicated throughout the world. But there might be a few people who aren't familiar with it.

Beverley: Ready or Not was the first real tween show of its kind. It was a high-quality show, written and produced with humor and integrity. Even today, my daughter is still recognized, almost seventeen years after the show was being broadcast. In many ways, she has been given the chance to see what a little bit of fame can bring. Some of these times you don't want to be recognized and to have to answer questions like: "What are you doing now?"

It was a great time, but it can be a difficult past to carry forward from childhood into adulthood. Of course, her teen years were not lived in the same way as anyone else she knew. She missed a lot of the socializing that happens as a teen. She was schooled on set and when she was not on set, she attended an arts high school, where at times her peers made it very difficult for her. She still has some good friends she made in those days, thank goodness.

We often talk about the toll that celebrity takes on privacy and how it is a trade-off, because it seems the public believes that they are entitled to every little bit of their favorite celebrity's life. Lani would tell you, the attention and the constant scrutiny can at times become a burden. So, absolutely, many of my best times have been with her in relation to her overall life experiences, and I think and hope she might have a few memories of mine that she has been a part of. We're like the two musketeers off to share adventures.

Erings: Well, I certainly can relate to the privacy issue in my life—or lack of it, I must say! Thanks for that peek into your daughter's world. I know you have lots more to say about Lani in the book. I'd love for you to tell the viewers about, as you call it, your surreal chance to meet pop artist Peter Max. Your daughter was with you on that one, too.

Beverley: Well, I have been a big, big fan of Peter Max's art since I first became aware of him in the '60s. He was the artist of our generation. The joy, the bold colors, the cosmic imagery, even the psychedelia of his work, was kind of the backdrop or landscape of our generation. He has been an extremely prolific artist, his images appearing on everything from jumbo airplanes to clothing to book covers to his own canvases. His famous "Love" image has always been one of my favorites. I had already been fortunate enough to purchase a 1970's piece of his at an auction. The piece called *American Lady* remains a cherished possession of mine.

His artwork has now become extremely expensive. I tried to buy more Max pieces at auction, but they were getting increasingly out of reach for me, price-wise. I was able to get several more pieces, including a re-issue of that famous "Love" image, which I was ecstatic about. Max is prolific and very Libran in his images. He is also a dynamic marketer. Peace and love and harmony. I think of those things when I see Max's work.

Erings: Yes, Peter Max is an icon in the pop-art world, I'd say.

Beverley: He absolutely is. So, in 2002, when I heard a local Toronto gallery was hosting a Peter Max exhibit that included a special appearance by the man himself, I couldn't contain myself. In his entire career, he had never been to Canada before. I found that unbelievable, so I was determined I would not let the opportunity escape me. I had to meet Max. I still owned a long-sleeved shirt from one of his clothing lines—I think from the '70s—which I never wore but kept as another piece of his art. I decided I would take it with me in hopes that he might autograph it or something. The "something" turned out to be more than I could ever have expected.

We arrive at the gallery and they are not allowing anything, absolutely nothing, into the premises, other than physical bodies. Peter Max's wishes. It is for security, we're told.

It is a smallish gallery, long and narrow, and I'm initially very happy we are early enough to get in. However, I must take this shirt in with me. This is the first and only time I can remember that I might have been referred to as a "smuggler" and actually didn't care. I remember that I stuffed the shirt under my coat. I was still very thin, so no one would suspect anything. Being near the front of the line, it didn't take long until we were in.

Erings: Who else were you with?

Beverley: My daughter and her artist friend. We are perusing the exhibition. I'm vocally oohing and awing and telling my daughter which of the pieces I would purchase if I could afford it. She tells me her favorites. And then, the magic moment. In walks Peter Max with his small entourage of assistants. He has a bold elegance about him as he cruises into the center of the room. I take a few moments before I muster up the courage, and am gently pushed with encouragement, by my daughter and her friend, to make a move toward him.

Erings: What was your reluctance?

Beverley: Well, I always have great ideas and can envision the scenario, but deep down inside I'm basically quite shy. And I'm in awe of this iconic man.

However, I take a deep breath, muster my courage and make my way to Peter Max, joining the line for my turn to have a moment with him. My moment arrives and I proceed, with great originality, to tell him how much I love his work. I bet he's never heard that before!

My daughter's friend is talking to him about acrylics and chatting about art-related things. He is very engaging, but I can sense our time is running out. Before he has a chance to move on to the next original line of conversation with some other admirer, I decide I must pull out the shirt. I proceed to do it with somewhat of a dramatic flare. His eyes open very wide when he sees it. He summons his assistant. They examine the label to ensure it is the real deal. They quickly confirm that it is.

She tells me that Peter Max would like to know if I would like to trade the shirt, as he is planning to open a Peter Max Museum in New York, and this would be an item that would fit into the future museum's contents.

"Trade for what?" I ask.

She tells me it is my shirt for an original, hand-drawn, black-and-white, personalized and signed piece of artwork by Peter Max. I'm sure my mouth opened widely as I stood looking at her in utter disbelief.

Again, most people would have jumped at this chance, but I asked if I could think about it. Before I actually moved away to think, I asked if he could add an additional color to the black. You never know unless you ask.

So off she goes, scrambling around for another marker and returning to tell me they had found a red one. Still not sure, I need another moment to think it over. I ask if they will grant me some additional time.

I really *loved* the shirt, even though it had only been on a hanger for twenty-odd years. I walk back to my daughter and her friend and ask the ridiculous question, "What I should do?"

"Mother, are you kidding me, how can you even ask me that question...Trade The Shirt!" is something like what she replied.

But, I still wasn't sure. "Why are you even asking me then?" she said. "Sometimes I don't understand you at all. An original Peter Max for a shirt?" She asked it in a question to make me see how ridiculous I sounded.

"Okay, I get it." I said.

Erings: You must have *really* loved the shirt!

Beverley: (smiling) Yes, Erings, I really loved the shirt! More deep thought, much pondering and a few minutes later, I tell his assistant that I am ready to trade the shirt. I am brought over to a small table, kind of a mini Max workspace, equipped with photocopy paper and two magic markers. They obviously had not come prepared for Peter Max to produce artwork that day! I stand beside him. That alone was surreal. He asks what images of his I like. Do I have a preference? *Definitely not the Statue of Liberty*, one of his popular images, I'm thinking, but I don't say that.

I tell him I love his women in profile and his hearts. Bang! No time to change my mind. He is in action. Boom, boom. A line, a curve. Both markers in the same hand, even. I am feeling like I may float away and out of my body. It is definitely one of those moments you want to remember every detail of, hold it and savor it, but somehow it is slipping away, in spite of you.

Erings: It still sounds like you remember it clearly.

Beverley: It honestly seemed to be over before I knew it. The whole thing took *maybe* a grand total of two minutes. But, I now possessed an eight-by-ten, photocopy-paper original, personalized and signed Peter Max. I confess there was a moment of sadness that I'd never again see the shirt, but I knew I would get over it. I vowed to visit it at his museum in New York.

Erings: Okay, so, what did you do with your original Peter Max? (an image of the framed piece projects up on the screen behind us and the audience oohs and ahs, like I do when I see Max artwork)

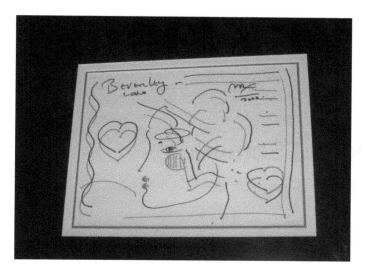

Original personalized Peter Max – Photocopy paper and markers, 2002

Beverley: As you can see, I had it framed and it now officially hangs in my bedroom. At first, I wished he hadn't personalized it, but now I'm glad he did.

Erings: Yes, I'm glad for you that he did! Fun story. Tell us, are you over the shirt yet?

Beverley: (smiling) I think so.

Erings: Great reminder of the colorful surprises life bring us when we're willing to let go. L-O-V-E it!

Stay tuned, because after these messages, we'll be right back on the spiritual path with Beverley Golden—seeking *and* finding out what it really means to be a hippie.

Seek and Sometimes Ye Shall Find

Erings: Based on the way you talk and write, I sense you've always had a rich spiritual life. It must have been part of your world from an early age.

Beverley: I appreciate that, but not really. In fact, I remember my brother once commenting that I had no connection to the spiritual part of my being. I was in my twenties, I believe, and I didn't really get what he was saying. At that time, I still equated spirituality with the religious connotation, which of course it has little to do with. I don't remember being too spiritual until I read Shirley MacLaine's book, *Out On A Limb,* in my early thirties.

Erings: Wow. I remember reading that, too! It was somewhat of a groundbreaker at the time for many of us.

Beverley: For sure. Well, back to your question about being spiritual from an early age. I do have several strong memories from about the age of twelve. I once wrote a protest letter to *Glamour* magazine about the inequality between the sexes. Of course, it didn't get published. Maybe the topic didn't suit their editorial content, but I loved the magazine. It was the first time I attempted to write for a larger audience. It was also my first rejection letter.

The spiritual side of my twelve-year-old equation was me thinking somehow it didn't make sense that we live for seventy-four years and there is nothing after that. You die and that's it? How come some people had such difficult lives and others had it seemingly easy? How was this fair?

The questioning went on and on and really stuck with me from that early age. It is the questioning, I'd like to believe, that made me a spiritual seeker. An unaware one, but a seeker all the same.

Erings: Great that you recognize that.

Beverley: In my twenties, I was reading books like *I'm Okay, You're Okay, Psychic Discoveries Behind the Iron Curtain,* and anything on astrology. The '70s introduced me to all these new ideas, and of course the women's movement was born then, too.

I believe this minimal exposure to spirituality contributed to my mind/body disconnect. I focused heavily on the mind part. I was quite materialistic and didn't seem to understand the connection of mind and body. It does seem rather unthinkable, unbelievable for me now, that I had little conscious connection to my spirituality. My parents were more religious than spiritual, and to this day my wonderful mother thanks God for everything. "You're home safe. Thank God." It works for her.

Erings: Yes, it works for a lot of people. So tell me, how did Shirley MacLaine's book fit in?

Beverley: Well, once I read it, I was on the path. Never turned back. My spiritual experiences kept escalating from there and propelled me forward. I believe it was part of our generation as well. In astrology, many things are common to a particular generation, so you see a definite pattern or sense of what is happening emerge. It was the Pluto-in-Leo, Gemini-in-Uranus, and Neptune-in-Libra generation.

Erings: Explain.

Beverley: Okay, briefly. Pluto in Leo can bring deep-reaching transformation in the self-image of human beings and their possibilities of self-development. This is the Boomer generation. Uranus in Gemini brings freedom of opinion, thought and speech. And, Neptune in Libra helps dissolve old forms of relationships and the previous understanding of art, bringing an idealization of peacefulness, love and art. So my interpretation is that we were the peace, love and groovy generation looking for some new and higher meaning to our lives. The generation of the seekers. Self-individuation and revolution were the key themes, too.

Erings: Okay, I can relate to that.

Beverley: In fact, since the early '70s, I have opened most conversations that appeared to be going anywhere, with either "what sign are you?" or "when were you born?" Although the Sun sign is only one basic indicator of a person, I have gotten to know certain markers of each sign that often appear when I observe people.

I find the astrology chart quite a fascinating tool to see who the individual has come here to be on its journey in this particular lifetime. And how they can transform it as well. Our birth charts are meant to teach us about who we are and who we can become. Life is, after all, about ongoing transformation.

Erings: I like that. Life is about ongoing transformation.

Beverley: I personally have had many astrology readings of my birth chart throughout the years, and without exception, I have been told that I have the chart of a writer, a communicator. In a way, I believe that is what I've always done. The trick for me is always how to tell these seemingly unbelievable stories in a humorous, yet realistic and relatable way.

Erings: You certainly have been able to do that! I must say you also seem extremely comfortable talking to groups. A lot of people, even people who make their living being in front of people, are not comfortable. In fact, they're timid with so much attention placed on them.

Beverley: Thank you, Erings. That's reassuring, considering that if I paused to think about the magnitude of this right now, I might freeze.

Erings: (winks) I don't think so.

Beverley: Well, I was a child of the '60s and I got my sea legs *and* my wings during this time. I remember when the stage play *Hair* first came out. We were moving into the Age of Aquarius and the play struck a deep chord with me. It really resonated with my beliefs. I hoped we as human beings were finally getting the larger picture. I had already seen *Hair* in London, England, L.A. and San Francisco.

My friend and I actually ushered at the theatre in San Francisco, as we had connected with the show's stage manager. It seemed like a fun thing to do. We act as ushers and get to see the show for free. We did this for several nights, so I really got to *see* the show. One night, we ended up back at the group house of the stage manager and others and we slept on the living-room floor. It was like a large orgy without any sex. I had enough issues with relationships, so free love in a group setting would definitely not have been for me.

When I heard that *Hair* would be auditioning for a Toronto cast, I was enormously excited and ready to audition. I planned to attend these open auditions. They began on Tuesday, October 21, 1969, to be exact. As a business marketing student, I decided I had to go to the open call, as shy as I was about performing in front of people. I brought my security blanket, in the form of my pitch pipe, which I had with me at all music-related events, hoping that somehow this would give me the confidence I needed.

Erings: Interesting that you were willing to audition, in spite of knowing what you would be asked to do if you got a part in the play. What was that experience like for you?

Beverley: When I got to the audition site, it appeared that thousands of us had shown up. In fact, the grand total was seven hundred fifty-five. Only ten professionals, who were given priority, showed up to audition on the first day. In total, only a hundred people got to audition on the first non-professional audition day. I wasn't one of them.

The day was very long. Bodies were everywhere; floors and stairs were all packed with *Hair* hopefuls. Enough hopefuls had shown up to fill more than a week's worth of auditions. Two huge semicircles of people sat facing the stage. Our energy created a calm atmosphere of peace and patience.

Erings: Another opportunity to practice patience.

Beverley: Absolutely. Day two, would however, be my chance. I was very excited, but I guess I hadn't really dressed the part. I was wearing a long fall (remember hair pieces called falls?) and a cool dress I'd bought in San Francisco. Someone told me I looked more like I should be on the *Tonight Show* than in *Hair.*

It didn't sound particularly like a positive omen and was my first clue that maybe I didn't look the part. I had also chosen to sing *Walk on By,* Dionne Warwick's hit song, which was probably another omen that I might not even be in the right musical genre for *Hair.* Personally, I had grown up listening to Steve and Edie, Sammy Davis Jr., Nancy Wilson and Joe Williams. But I did go ahead and sing and I believe I sounded good. Friends I had made waiting told me that I didn't seem nervous at all and my voice projected and I sang convincingly well. However, sadly, I was not asked to join the cast.

Erings: Overall, it does sound like a positive experience.

Beverley: Yes, and well, I guess there is one plus for standing out in the crowd, because I was interviewed outside by a well-known entertainment reporter. Naturally he asked me about the famous nude scene that had come to be symbolic of what *Hair* stood for. I would never have been comfortable doing it, but I told him I would have.

The "Hair" audition look, 1969

My exact words, in my big interview, were: "A lot of people here don't know what the play's about. I'm not the type to go really wild. I'd just like to be an entertainer. For instance, the nude scene. People shouldn't make this a major issue. It's just part of *Hair.*" That's what I said; could I have sounded any more glib, any more ridiculous?

Erings: You really remember what you said?

Beverley: Actually, Erings, I kept the newspaper article. (smiling) You never know when you'll need to be reminded of how you talked in the '60s.

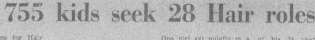

755 kids seek 28 Hair roles

Open auditions for Hair were held yesterday at the Rock Pile.

The auditions, in themselves, bore a similarity to what the "tribal love rock musical" is all about.

After the relatively quiet day of auditions for professionals on Friday — only 10 showed up — yesterday, with 755 kids registering for a chance to get into Hair, became an exercise in controlled chaos.

Only about 100 had a chance to sing yesterday, but there are enough applicants to keep the auditions going until Nov. 4th. From these, about 250 will be selected for a final audition before Hair's director, Tom

PETER GODDARD
MUSIC

O'Horgan, who will prune the show into its final size of 28 members. On Dec. 29, there will be given its first preview, the show opening for the public on January 11.

Although the process yesterday might have seemed rather slow, it was never painful. Waiting kids sat facing the stage in two huge semi-circles, one on the ground floor, one in the balcony.

At first, it looked as if Yorkville had just been shifted slightly east.

One girl sat quietly in a corner.

Are you going to audition?

"No, I don't think so," she said looking around. "Maybe . . . no, I don't think so."

"I really didn't want to be in it that much," said another, 15-year-old Maureen Marder. "Then I heard they're picking out kids just from the streets. Wow! — then I changed my mind."

Throughout all the proceedings there was a sense of community. In short, the auditions themselves were a groovy enough experience.

"You know, it felt very good being up there," said Mike Kennedy, who, having been a musician for seven

of his 24 years, seemed completely confident. "I want to have the right part in it. That's all."

A little less sure of herself after her audition, Beverley Golden thought "a lot of people here don't know what the play's about. I'm not the type to go really wild. I'd like just to be an entertainer. For instance, the nude scene. People shouldn't make this a major issue. It's just part of Hair."

"Well, I saw the nude scene in the London version of Hair," said Jacqueline Morrison, 17, waiting for her audition until next Monday. "It was done abstractly there. It was in context. It's the whole aura of Hair. It's just a thing I want to get into."

My big media interview after "Hair" audition, 1969

I had said it was no big deal, but I do wonder if I had gotten a part—would I have taken it all off? I thought, maybe they would have made an exception for me. I would be the only one to *not* take their clothes off.

Erings: I guess we'll never know. What happened after that?

Beverley: I went back to school *pumped* that I had actually gone through with the audition, and proceeded to audition for the school's yearly sketch comedy revue called *Riot*. It was written and performed by the Radio and Television Arts students. I got a part! I was the token non-RTA student, and I didn't even have to consider taking my clothes off. I got a chance to try to be funny too.

To finish off the *Hair* thing—when I did see the production in Toronto, the nude scene was done very tastefully, using low and discreet lighting. I believe some of the cast did get to keep their clothes on. I still love that show to this day.

Erings: *Hair* was and is great theatre. What did you learn from this experience and why was *Hair* so profound for you?

Beverley: For me, *Hair* represented a new possibility in both theatre and the world. It was considered rebellious, something entirely new in the theatre world. The topic and the rock-type score and the dialogue were revolutionary.

To me, *Hair* defined the '60s generation's search for meaning. It was the decade of "be-ins," "love-ins" and protests, and I see so clearly the parallels with today. Astrologically there was a strong Uranus-Pluto transit back then, as is occurring now—Uranus being the planet of revolution and unexpected sudden change, and Pluto the planet of transformation.

In many ways, *Hair* represented all I believed was possible. A world based on peace, not war. A world where the individual can speak up and be heard. To this day, I still see and hold that as the highest possibility for the future of this planet.

To live in a world of peace, both inner and outer, is what I have always envisioned as a real possibility. Now, more and more people are gathering and collaborating to hold this vision for our future.

Our sayings back then were "make love, not war" and "give peace a chance." Interesting that we are still facing the same challenges, yet in even bigger ways than we were back in the '60s and '70s. But I am eternally optimistic.

I see how I was, and still truly am, a hippie. I have always embodied the ideals that were so prevalent and alive back then—world peace, transformation, exploration, music, consciousness, compassion, community, spirituality, astrology, and of course one of the most powerful keywords for all generations...love.

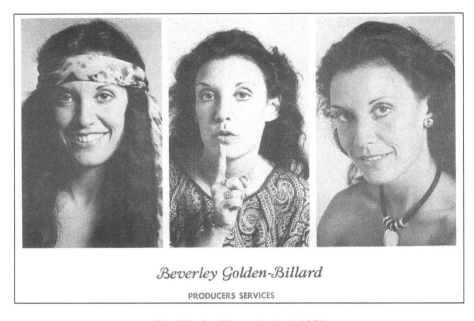

Beverley Golden-Billard

PRODUCERS SERVICES

The "Hippiest" I ever looked, 1976

Erings: Love *is* the answer! Thanks for reminding us all of those ideals by sharing that story. I know we have a lot of viewers who grew up in the '60s and '70s. Good times, but two decades of serious change and consciousness-raising. And I do see how the times we live in right now *are* absolutely running very parallel to back then.

Okay. The '80s are around the corner and the next segment will absolutely be about…Daryl Hall.

Past Lives, Reincarnation, Karmic Reunions and Daryl Hall

Erings: Beverley, you talk about reincarnation, past lives and karmic reunions quite a bit in your book—almost as if these are common experiences for all of us.

Beverley: (smiling) You mean they aren't, Erings?

I've definitely experienced quite a few times in my life when events or experiences led me to explore these as being real possibilities. I absolutely believe in reincarnation and now am a believer in the possibility of remembering our past lives and of actually becoming aware of relationships from those past lives as well. Relationships that play out, in this lifetime, as karmic reunions. Of course, awareness can help complete the unfinished karma.

I have come to understand that we do travel in soul groups. Often that means in this lifetime there is a group of five hundred people whom we might have had relationships with in previous lifetimes. Some people explain love at first sight as a karmic reunion of souls who recognize each other.

Erings: That's a sweet idea to consider. Tell us about that fascinating past-life regression experience when your daughter was young.

Beverley: Yes, Erings, my daughter and I had a most interesting experience with a past-life regression. I'm sure you are referring to the incident when Lani was seven. When you are seven and naïve and still trusting in a world that is a little bit crazy, you feel safe enough to yell out: "We're going to a party and we're going to be home REALLY LATE." I think having a mother who always wears rose-colored glasses doesn't help dispel that belief too easily either.

In this case, someone out in that wild and crazy world might have heard, because when we did arrive home that night—not so late really—our once secure home had been broken into and completely ransacked. Being there became extremely traumatic for her and even as time went on, the fear didn't subside. In her words, our house became "scary."

Erings: How did that play out?

Beverley: Well, Lani was afraid to be in the house and definitely wouldn't go into our basement unaccompanied. One day, we were sitting on the bed and she looked at me quite innocently and said, and these are her exact words, "Sometimes I think you're a burglar with my mommy's face on." What?? It didn't make much sense to me at the time. I continued to try to console her and assure her she didn't have to be concerned. However, there was something going on that she was just not going to let go of. She eventually refused to even go into the basement, at all.

In the meantime, we had been introduced, through our doctor, to a woman who did past-life regressions. We decided to try it. Maybe we'd uncover, and hopefully release, some of the fear my daughter was carrying—a fear that had become a burden. So we took my husband along with us and were ready to face whatever came up.

Erings: I must say that is very open-minded of you, Beverley!

Beverley: I guess so, Erings. I've always been open to try anything new. Although I was curious, I had no previous experience with this kind of work at all.

Erings: Now we're curious to hear how it all unfolded.

Beverley: My daughter and I lay beside each other on the woman's bed and she guided us into a kind of relaxed quasi-trance state. What happened was very immediate. We all saw the exact same scene at the same time. It was a large, turn-of-the-century Victorian-era mansion. I think it was London, England. One side of the house was brightly lit and people were laughing and dancing. A large and boisterous party was in progress.

The other side of the house was dark, and lurking outside in the shrubbery was a young man wearing a soft-brimmed cap with an empty satchel slung over his shoulder. He quietly slipped into the house through a partly open window and snuck up the narrow stairs to a second-floor bedroom. Upstairs was where all the guests' fur coats had been placed.

When he unexpectedly woke up a sleeping child, she screamed out in terror. The child had seen his face. We all recognized I was the young burglar lad and my daughter was the little girl he had startled. So now, "Sometimes I think you're a burglar with my mommy's face on" made perfect sense. It was quite a powerful experience to actually witness that. And we all saw it, even the woman facilitating the process.

Erings: Sounds somewhat unbelievable actually. So, did that clear your daughter's fears?

Beverley: To a degree. At least she didn't think I was a burglar anymore. She was young and it might have been hard to digest and process, but I was amazed and still wonder how we all saw the same scene at the same time. No power of suggestion. It was that vivid.

Erings: So interesting! Thanks for sharing that intimate peek into a past-life regression.

Jumping now from past lives to the present, I guess you know what is next. Beverley, what *IS* this thing you have with Daryl Hall of the pop duo Hall & Oates?

Beverley: I *knew* we were leading up to this, so I really will do my best to not come off sounding a bit...well, loopy. It is difficult to talk about because it went on for a very long time, and is very complicated for me to explain in words.

I think it began in the early '80s, when Hall & Oates first became highly visible on the music scene. I instantly loved their music, and I had this very strange attraction to Daryl Hall. (smiling) I mean, I'm sure lots of girls had a strange attraction to Daryl Hall. I felt like I knew him. It was as if I knew everything about him. It became quite a predominant obsession for me in my life. I was sure I was supposed to connect with him.

Everyone who knew me knew about this "love" I had for Daryl Hall—to the point that most of them thought of him when they thought of me. It was extremely intense for a very long time. I mean, by the end of the '80s, I didn't even quite understand this connection.

In 1991, Daryl Hall and John Oates were coming to Toronto. I pulled every string I had in the entertainment industry, which I was still a part of, to get backstage passes to meet him. A very good friend of mine already confirmed we had front row seats for the concert. He actually used his music-business connections and bought them for us. Truly incredible as this was, I was still determined to find a way to go backstage to the planned meet and greets, which are standard fan-type gatherings either before or after the show.

I had a single-minded goal: to get passes, no matter what. And, I did. I got before-the-show AND after-the-show backstage passes to "meet and greet" them. I was so intimidated that there wasn't much dialogue between us at all. My daughter was a cute little girl and we all got to take pictures with Daryl and John.

Before we even got to the theatre, I had envisioned that Daryl would be wearing a black and white shirt.

Erings: And?

Beverley: Indeed, he was. I don't know why that's particularly important, but it was some kind of confirmation of being tuned in to him. It is funny how no one knew for sure who we were, so our pictures took a long time to make it to us. I looked like a frightened deer-in-the-headlights caught in the spotlight, but I had pictures with him.

Erings: It doesn't end there though, does it?

Beverley: No, it was actually a prelude to what was to follow. Later in the '90s, my ex Doug and I, with two close friends who were also musicians, wrote a song specifically for them and hoped to get it to Daryl and John. We had one of the best local session singers perform the song. Amazing vocals that sounded much like Daryl Hall. Daryl Hall is one of pop's premiere singers known for his pure blue-eyed soul vocals.

In a big concert coming up at Canada's Wonderland, Daryl Hall and John Oates were going to be performing with Carly Simon. Fabulous bill. We had the demo with us and hoped to call on a music-biz connection to get the song to him. He told us he would; but with this guy, I had my doubts.

So naturally I took matters into my own hands. The concert was amazing, and after the show we looked for our connection to see if he would get us backstage. We hung out for what seemed like an eternity…and with the crowd almost gone, the amphitheatre area was virtually empty. It was getting close to park closing time as well and we were still hanging out at the entrance to the backstage area. Lani was antsy to leave.

Suddenly, an unfamiliar man came to the gate that separated the seats from backstage. As luck would have it, he recognized my daughter from her TV series and started to talk to us.

We told him what had happened with the song and he said he didn't think it was given to anyone involved with the group. He just *happened* to be the Hall & Oates tour manager. Seriously! He brought us backstage, but everyone had left from there as well. We went from trailer to trailer looking, but no one was left in the backstage area. He then suggested we come down to the hotel the guys were staying at and hang out with them. He told us they would be in the hotel bar.

Erings: Would you call that synchronicity?

Beverley: Absolutely! Synchronicity makes things that simple. *I* almost couldn't believe it happened so easily. I was so very nervous. My eighteen-year-old daughter remained cool and cavalier. It was I, after all, who was propelling this forward. Lani wouldn't have cared at all if we went home—and said so several times as we drove downtown.

As we approached the hotel, I didn't know if I could handle the terror and excitement I was feeling. I'm sure I stopped breathing several times, but I just kept moving forward. This was, for me, the chance of a lifetime.

We walked through the lobby to the bar and luckily the tour manager was close to the door. He smiled and said he was hoping we'd come. He welcomed us in and there we were. Almost face to face with Daryl, Charlie DeChant and T-Bone Wolk.

They didn't really take much notice of us until I made a comment that Barry Manilow happened to be playing in town this night as well. Daryl commented, "Oh yeah, Barry Manilow?" and as the saying goes...let the conversation begin. I don't remember any of the topics we talked about, but it was *very* easy, as if we had known each other forever—like a casual, comfortable conversation between longtime friends.

Erings: You do seem to be good at that, Beverley. Any surprises?

Beverley: Not to me, really. We ended up going back to their room, hung out and pretty much talked and talked. I felt like I was reuniting with someone I had known long ago and still knew, but who didn't know me. It was a really amazing night. It was just talk and laughs, nothing else.

Friends insinuated that I'd blown my chance. The tour manager very visibly showed that he liked Lani, and wouldn't that have been a story to tell? Mother and daughter. (laughing) I don't even want to think about it. Instead we got the tour manager's card and said our goodbyes. It was almost unbelievably casual and easy. That's about all I can say.

Erings: But that wasn't the last time you'd see him?

Beverley: No, Erings, it definitely was not. But let me first tell you about a specific part of the book written about their early years. *Dangerous Dances* by Nick Tosches includes a story I was very struck by. In the book is the following quote: "Daryl shared with John his notion that they had been leaders of the Spanish Inquisition in another lifetime and were now paying for their heinous deeds of long ago centuries."

This book came out in September 1984 before their tour to promote their album *War Babies*. When I read that, my body tingled, which often means something is resonating as the truth. Was it possible that I had lived a life with them back then as well? The moment that I read that, I somehow recognized it as the reason for the connection. I obviously have no way of proving that, but you never know!

Erings: No, you never do know. So when did you meet up with them again?

Beverley: A year or so later, Daryl and John were playing at the local fairgrounds. It was a night of torrential rains and the venue itself was not easily accessible without a lengthy walk across a large grassy, muddy field. In my opinion, it was not a concert venue worthy of them. Because it was an outdoor concert, the audience was thoroughly drenched.

There was no cover of any kind. Lani and I were determined—well, more like I was determined—to go to the show. I don't do rain very well, so I envisioned another plan to avoid sitting in the audience. Soaked to the bone, we approached what looked like the backstage access entrance, where I boldly asked for DL, the stage manager we met the year before. I showed his business card, thinking this would be the proof that we knew him.

Coincidentally, someone else I knew from the music business was also backstage and I'm sure he was surprised to see me and my daughter trying to get in. So the person looked at the business card, while I inhaled a deep breath praying this would work. I didn't even know if he was still the tour manager. The guy said, "Okay, I'll call him for you." "Were in!" I thought. And we were in.

Like famous VIPs, we were ushered backstage to the green room. I looked like a drowned rat by then and had a lot of pain in my gut. Nothing new, but really bad timing. It was almost unbearable, but I had gotten this far and I was not turning back. I had to try to make friends with my pain.

We hung out for a while in the makeshift green room and people were looking at us, wondering who we were. Then, we were brought to a backstage area and literally got to sit on the floor backstage and watch the concert. In spite of the intense pain, which I experienced so often, I had to grin and bear it in order to stay in the experience and enjoy it. Some of my pain memories actually still take my breath away.

Erings: I've never had severe pain personally, so I'm still not sure how people can walk around with that much pain. I guess somehow it must become a part of your life.

Beverley: Unfortunately, yes to that. In this case, it was probably a once-or-twice-in-a-lifetime opportunity, so what choice do you make? I had missed a lot of my life succumbing to the pain, and this wasn't going to be one of those nights!

The show was fantastic. Maybe even more so from our backstage vantage point. The whole crew is questioning this choice of venue and who booked it for them. In great weather, it would have been fabulous. I know all this because after the show, we traipsed back across the now even muddier and soggier field and met up with them at the hotel again. Straight to their room this time. Very innocent intentions, but straight to their room.

Erings: Almost unbelievable when you stop to consider the facts.

Beverley: I never looked at it that way. Here we are, hanging out again talking about life and relationships; again, it was casual and easy. I was lying on my side, perched on one arm, on the floor of the bedroom, still trying to deal with the pain. In some ways, the scene was a bit surreal. How do you explain lying on the floor of Daryl Hall's hotel bedroom and talking, looking up at him sitting on his bed? While trying to survive being drenched and in exhausting pain, pretending like not much is happening inside my turmoiled gut.

I did a pretty good job, too, I must admit. It was a great night. For me, anyways. My daughter was probably bored, but she did it for me. In some ways, she was part of the ticket in from the first time we met.

Erings: Who else was there this time?

Beverley: All the other guys from the band were also there, in the adjoining room, watching television and just hanging out. For all the longtime Daryl Hall and John Oates fans, it is a well-known fact that they basically have had the same players for years. It was a great group, including T-Bone Wolk on bass and many other instruments, Charlie "Mr. Casual" DeShant on sax and keyboards, and Mike Braun on drums.

Sadly, T-Bone Wolk passed away in late February 2010, while apparently working on a solo album with Daryl. The news stunned me, as he was such a key player with the group. All of these guys had their own unique style and charisma and are great, great players.

Erings: You really seem to know a lot about them. And of course about Daryl Hall. Tell us more about what happened.

Beverley: On this particular night, I really felt I *hadn't* been imagining anything; I really knew this person, even though he didn't know me. Later, I started having these dreams, and I was pretty sure that there was some strong soul connection from a previous life or maybe some unfinished karma. I'm sure it does sound a bit preposterous; but unless you have experienced it, it is almost impossible to explain.

Erings: Would you tell us about the dreams?

Beverley: Well, they were intense dreams, a strong indication that ours was beyond an earthly connection. They weren't the average romantic or sexual dreams, but rather like two people living a life together in an alternative dimension.

These types of dreams are supportive in nature—it is almost like an "I see you" interaction where you just "get" each other. I believe that is what a soul connection is. I am not someone who knows much about dream interpretation. I've read that some people, who are authorities on dreams, believe that each person in your dream represents a part of yourself. I dare to say, these aren't those kinds of dreams, if you understand what I mean. It is virtually impossible to put into words. It does sound a bit unbelievable I'm sure, but sometimes I wake up exhausted because it feels so real. I feel like I've lived a whole day in the dream.

It reminds me of a *Twilight Zone* episode where a man is having two parallel lives, his real one and his dream one. By the end of the episode, neither he nor the audience knows which is real and which is not. I do know that this is my real world, but that is almost the sense I have at times. Sorry if I'm not able to describe it well; but again, unless you have experienced something like it, you can't put earthly words to it.

Erings: So, is it more of a feeling, or do you see visuals?

Beverley: Both. In the dreams, it is definitely me and it is definitely him. A lot of the dreams are set in a music scenario and in a few I have woken up remembering songs we were writing together. I've never remembered the entire song, but I have a few titles that I've written down. Most of the time, John Oates is there too, and he always recognizes me.

Erings: Which would make sense if you three shared a previous lifetime together, as you believe. I don't know how possible it is, but I do believe in the same things that you do regarding past lives and reincarnation.

Beverley: Yes, it does make perfect sense to me. As I mentioned, I am not in any way an expert on dreams, but my understanding is that our soul leaves our body when we sleep—so for me, it is like our souls are reuniting and we are having a soul encounter. In one dream, he actually said he had been dreaming about me, but didn't know who I was.

In another dream, I got daring and asked him if we were together or not. His reply was something like, "I'm with you when I'm there." I remember waking up and asking myself, "Where exactly is there? How do I know how to get there? Do I need to relocate?" Of course there is a Buddhist saying, "Wherever you go, there you are." So in my dreams is the "there." For me, this is a soul experience, where I'm me and he is him, and "there" is in my dreams. It definitely feels otherworldly.

Erings: So, that's it? Have you seen him again?

Beverley: Sure. I go to his concerts when they come to town and I always have the same feeling: I know this person. I sometimes feel what he is feeling and think what he is thinking, or that is the way it seems to me. Of course we can never feel or think the way another person does, but we can get pretty close. Can't explain more than that. I'm sure it does sound...well whatever word you want to put there.

Erings: Would you like the chance to reconnect again, given the opportunity?

Beverley: (looking around) You are not going to surprise me here are you, Erings?

Erings: No. No. Would I do that?

Beverley: Well, you have been known to surprise your guests.

But of course I would. However, it has been a long time and so much has happened in both or our lives that I have to trust that if it is supposed to happen, it will happen.

Erings: Very Zen. This isn't the only such karmic reunion with someone from another lifetime though, is it?

Beverley: No. There was another really big one. Also in the late '90s, I became what has been termed as a "*Rent* junkie." Not since *Hair* in the '70s, had a piece of musical theatre so resonated and impacted me. My daughter and I were serious *Rent* heads. I think altogether we have each seen the show at least twenty-two times. Maybe even more. My daughter and I became part of the group who would hang out, or have someone hang out for us, to get the twenty-dollar front row seats.

I must add that one of my daughter's friends, from her television days, had a leading role in *Rent*; so we kind of knew people and certainly all the cast of the production knew who my daughter was. I think I mentioned Lani is highly recognizable, didn't I? Anyhow, this show touched me in a very profound way. Even seeing it again recently, again sitting in the second row, we absolutely loved it. For me, it is a brilliant piece of theatre. It touches on all the emotions one feels when in deep and sincere personal relationships. And how love and loss, even though a part of our life as human beings, can be exuberant at times and painful and sad at others. The story of Jonathan Larson creating this magical piece of musical theatre, and then dying on the eve of the final dress rehearsal, also touched me very deeply. But the baby he birthed, *Rent,* got to live on.

Erings: I have heard some people say that not since *Hair* had there been a comparable musical-theatre experience until *Rent* appeared. So, it makes sense that both of these incredible pieces of theatre would be so moving to you. (smiling) But it wasn't just about the play of course, was it?

Beverley: No, Erings, there was something much more profound in store for me. I think as early as the first time I saw it, I noticed and was drawn to one of the cast members. At first, I thought it was just that he was breathtakingly beautiful and I must be having this middle-age cougar thing stirring in me. However, it would turn out that it wasn't just that.

I asked my daughter's girlfriend about him, if he had a girlfriend and so on. I might add that he was very young, gifted and black. I personally had never had much exposure to black people. I was certainly curious about their culture and their history as a people. But one-to-one, not too much contact.

One night, Lani and I were hanging out backstage and I started to talk to him. It happened very casually and easily. The next thing I know, he is asking me for my phone number and saying he'll call me. I was quite shocked, but he did get my number. (smiling) In a lot of ways.

Erings: And he called?

Beverley: He did call. The first time he called, it was a bit late at night for me, and I remember asking if we could talk tomorrow or whenever. What was I thinking? I already knew I wasn't going to sleep after that call, so I might as well have talked to him. My heart was smiling.

He did call again and we set up a dinner date; but I was a bit perplexed, not at all sure what this could be about. He seemed older, somehow. I thought he was around thirty, but he was much younger than that. He had a very old presence. We met backstage after a Sunday matinee. Backstage is kind of outside and behind the theatre, so it isn't very private.

We greet each other from across the street with a smile. My heart is both pounding and bursting. He is drop-dead gorgeous. He takes my breath away, if that is possible for a man to have that effect on a woman.

Erings: (winks) I would say that is possible.

Beverley: I feel as nervous as a teenager with a serious crush, going on a first date. When my daughter's friend sees me and him, she looks at me and cheers, "Way to go Beverley!" I'm sure I smiled. He had no idea what she meant.

Erings: Maybe it's a woman kind of thing.

Beverley: Maybe. Anyhow, we have a great Thai food dinner. As we talk, I realize that he is very intense; but when he smiles, he is breathtaking.

Erings: So, did you…?

Beverley: Yes, Erings, I asked him when his birthday was, as I thought this might go somewhere. Turns out he's a Scorpio with Libra rising, a pretty deadly combo for me. In an attraction kind of way. Any Libra with Scorpio or Scorpio with Libra is pretty irresistible for me. Daryl Hall was one of the first with this combination to impact me. He's a Libra with Scorpio rising.

Of course I asked him how old he was. When he said twenty-two, I think my jaw might have dropped and my heart skipped a beat, backward. Oh my God! I'm forty-eight and he's less than half my age. I've suddenly gone from being a cougar to being a cradle robber! What am I even thinking here?

When I commented that I thought he was older, he said he was aware of that and was confident he would grow into his age. With all of my emotions stirred, I was feeling extremely uncomfortable, out of any element I had ever been able to relate to. However, here we were.

Some would think it was a great opportunity to have a fling or whatever older women and younger men do, but that wasn't who I was. Sometimes I wish if only it could have been just that, it might have been a once-in-a-lifetime opportunity. *Rent* stayed in Toronto for a really long time. I went night after night with no sleep at all. It was so intense. All the time. I turned to meltable putty every time I was in his presence.

Erings: Did you have any more one-on-one interactions with him?

Beverley: (smiling) Oh, yes. I still remember the time I invited him to my house for dinner. Everyone was rooting for me, hoping that this would be the night. But I was not intending to go to that place. It was a really nice evening. We decided to watch the movie *Phenomenon,* me sitting on the floor, which I do quite a lot, and him on the couch.

When it came to the part in the movie where John Travolta's and Kyra Sedgwick's characters are having a picnic, I knew what was coming, but he hadn't seen the film. So Kyra Sedgwick's character says something to the effect, "Are you thinking you might get lucky tonight?" And exactly in sync with John Travolta, my friend says, "Just hoping." Almost as if he intuitively knew what was coming. Oh God. It was a moment when I really wished I *knew* what to do. But, I didn't, so I did nothing. Again. Lost opportunity?

Erings: Well, you can't say you don't have opportunities! Then what?

Beverley: We continued this kind of see-each-other friendship for the duration of *Rent* in Toronto. Finally, after about eight months, *Rent* was leaving and going to Vancouver. I was trying to prepare for the fact that he was leaving soon and maybe I'd never see him again. I was lying outside on a beautiful July day, a Sunday morning. I was feeling a lot of sadness and heaviness. From seemingly out of nowhere, I was viewing a very specific scene behind my closed eyes. I felt no real attachment to it. It just started playing out like a short movie.

It appeared to be during Medieval Times—although I'm definitely not a history expert, so that's just a hunch. I sensed it was a time of kingdoms and kings. I saw a man dressed in regal robes, riding a horse across a vast expanse of open plains. A woman was sitting behind him, holding on to his waist as he was speeding forward. Suddenly an arrow pierced the man's heart and he fell off the horse. He had been killed. The woman was overly distraught.

That is what I saw, but then unexpectedly for sure, I began to cry and cry. For about two hours, I continued sobbing. It was painful and coming from a deep place. I realized that I was the woman and he was the man. He was older and white. I was quite young and had cocoa colored skin. I revisited the scene and saw how much we had loved each other. He was a man of stature and power and I was a student. On the surface, to our faces, people had appeared to accept our love; but behind our backs, we were scorned. I was not considered good enough for a man of his status.

We loved to dance together and people would stop to watch us as we commanded the dance floor. I believe we were leaving our home to make a new life somewhere. That's when he was killed. He had always protected me and we had a mutual respect and love for each other. In some ways in this lifetime, we both have never let our hearts be open since. He was physically scarred in his heart and I emotionally. It felt like a great, great love that I guess a soul never forgets. An unfulfilled love. So, our souls had recognized each other again this time around. I had no idea what to do with this.

Erings: You got all that from just the scene coming up?

Beverley: It was pouring out of me. I was doing my own past life regression without even knowing it, or even knowing that I knew how! It was so very clear to me. I was very moved by what had happened. I really wanted to share it with him, but it was a delicate situation because I didn't think in any way he would get it.

Erings: Wow! So, did you ever tell him?

Beverley: Absolutely. He wasn't quite at the place in his life where he might fully understand it. He made a comment referring to the Erica Badu song with the line, "See you next lifetime." I have to think he got it on some small level.

Erings: So *Rent* leaves Toronto, and that's it? You never see him again?

Beverley: Not exactly. It wasn't over just yet. The production, as I mentioned, was moving to Vancouver…and it just so happened that Lani and I were making a trip to B.C., to visit my brother.

Of course, I planned to reconnect with all these friends from the cast. We got our tickets and hung out; this time "backstage" is in the front lobby and everyone is very happy to see us. Hugs and "Oh! So great to see you guys" all around. Then I see him. Again my heart kind of skips a beat. I try to take a breath and all the feelings are back again.

We do agree to have dinner together. It will be me, him, Lani and another mutual male friend from the cast. I felt it was safer for me and him—well maybe just me—to have these chaperones. Nothing has really changed for me. I'm as nervous as a teenager. I can't speak as cohesively or intelligently as I believe I'm normally capable of. I do have a wonderful picture of us that was taken at dinner in the restaurant. I still smile when I see it, but the feelings from then have dissipated and are part of the past for me.

Erings: And something else happened that day as well?

Beverley: Yes, perhaps the most interesting part of that day was when we were walking back from the restaurant to the theatre in downtown Vancouver. A gentleman, who was trying to collect money for a kids' shelter, approaches us and asks innocently if we are husband and wife. He says, "NO." We give the man some money.

Then the man persists and asks if we are boyfriend and girlfriend. This time I laugh and say no. I'm trying to clock what he is thinking. But, the man isn't giving up and he asks, "Lovers?" "No," we say in unison. "None of those."

The stranger says, "Well, you are definitely something." Yes, I think. We definitely are, or were, something. Then, that was it.

Of course my daughter and I are friends with him on Facebook, but he remains very private and only shares things about his theatre or television gigs. Although I initially sent him birthday cards and stayed in touch, I have no contact with him at all now. I believe in some ways a little bit of that past karma might have been fulfilled and cleared, just by virtue of us connecting again in this lifetime.

Erings: You seem to have fairly vivid memories of a lot of these events in your life. Do you have any other stories along these lines? Past lives or anything else you might be willing to tell us about?

Beverley: Nothing as specific or profound as these stories, but there are a couple to do with my ex-husband. I think I mentioned he had been a prominent lead singer with a popular Canadian band, soon after we had met. I remember the time they went on tour to the Southern United States, with New Orleans as one of their stops. I was pretty new in the relationship and still feeling insecure about how our relationship might go. After all, he was a lead singer in a rock-and-roll band; and having heard a lot of his pre-me stories, I knew that lead singers never have a difficult time finding a warm female to take them home for the night. So, I had some fears, or at least concerns.

For the first few days, he called me daily. But, sometime after that, I lost touch with him. He didn't call. I couldn't reach him in the hotel and I was, in my typical way back then, in minor-panic mode. I imagined every scenario you can conjure up. The worst was that he had shacked up with some cute little Southern belle and I was now ancient history.

Erings: You really invented that after only a few days of being out of touch?

Beverley: Did I mention that I have a very active mind, Erings? Of course, it was just my overblown imagination. He had been faithful—the Aunt Jemima toaster cover he brought me as a gift would later prove that. He had just been out enjoying the culture and rich musical history of the city *and* buying me a gift. I still don't think he had any idea what it really was, unless he was into giving very practical gifts. I actually didn't even have a toaster!

When he finally did call, I was relieved and he told me some of the stories of the group's adventures. There was the all-black university gig with only a handful of audience members who obviously had no idea who they were! They played their hearts out anyway. And the older black bellman in the hotel who said, "Yes sir. Yes ma'am," to everyone with a bowed head. It seemed hard to believe in this modern day that this kind of subservience still existed.

However, back to the part that relates to your original question, Erings. When Doug came home with the band, I went to the airport to pick him up. I clearly remember watching the band all coming toward me as I stood with the other partners who were waiting for their guys. I ran to greet him. I'm hugging him, he's hugging me, and in an instant "I" was hovering at the roof of the airport, looking down on the scene below. I knew that I was down on the ground physically hugging him, but the real "I," my soul, had travelled out of my body and was watching the scene from above. This is my one and only conscious experience of astral traveling. I have no idea how long I was out—I'm sure a fraction of a moment—or how I got back, but I did.

Erings: Wow. I've heard about it, but personally it hasn't happened to me. Can you talk about it a bit more?

Beverley: Back in the '60s and '70s, this idea of astral traveling was a topic for the seekers. I didn't know how to make it happen. In this instance, it just happened. I believe people were practicing the art of astral travel though. I must say that I still remember how incredibly light I felt and how trippy it was. The scary part was the "what if I don't come back?" feeling, but of course I did.

Erings: I'm sure people still do practice astral travel. I hear all the time about people and their out-of-body experiences, more in relation to near-death incidences though. I myself have never had that kind of experience and I admit I have had a lot of unusual experiences. So, you have one more incident that might be fun to hear about.

Beverley: Not as dramatic a story perhaps, but back in the '70s, Doug and I decided to buy a Ouija board to have some fun asking a few questions. We thought it would be a fun, "entertain your guests" kind of game. But let me tell you, it was definitely not a game in any way.

We were able to ask it lots of questions and we always thought we were getting answers, but we didn't know for sure if the answers had any truth to them. I mean, we were Ouija novices in a big way. So, there we were just playing with it for curiosity and a bit of fun. The session I most remember, or maybe it was a series of sessions, was when we asked it about "us" as a couple.

We stuck to questions like "Will we be together forever?" and relationship things in general. I guess being together forever isn't very general, but you get the idea. Then, we got daring. We decided to ask if we had been together in previous lives. Neither of us had any experience yet in seeing these lives, but we thought there was no harm in asking.

Well, the planchette or pointer went wild. It was like it had been waiting for us to ask and we had awoken a sleeping guide from the other side. Or something like that. We stuck with it, and through a series of questions we began to realize that maybe we had lived lots of lives before. No exact details, but just that we were soul mates who had agreed to reunite this time. I think to fulfill some karma together.

At that time it seemed very romantic; but when we split, the ugly stuff got in the way and I can only say I hope we did fulfill and resolve some karma. At the very least, we allowed our amazing daughter the ideal circumstance to come into the world for this lifetime of hers.

Erings: Any other Ouija experiences?

Beverley: Only that at one point a lot of years later, I found that Ouija board in the basement of my house and I had a strong sense I had to get rid of it. It spooked me out. Maybe I didn't like remembering what it had told me. I have always encouraged a friendship with my now ex and we are still able to be friends.

That's karma enough fulfilled. Exes who are friends. Works for me. More than what many can say, from what I see out in the world.

Erings: This is very true, Beverley. So do you think you two will be back together again in a future lifetime?

Beverley: I don't know. We both think we must have had major money issues in previous lifetimes—either together or apart—because in different ways, money has been a key issue for us both in this lifetime. I mean, this is a man who has bought the same numbers in the same lottery for thirty plus years and has never won a thing. He keeps hoping. My money issues are totally different.

Erings: Okay. Maybe we'll have time to come back to the money issue later. For now, let's take a short break and in our next segment we'll explore food and the profound effect it has had on your life. It's sure to be an interesting conversation and I, for one, am really looking forward to this topic.

Food, Glorious Food

Erings: Beverley, your book describes an incredible cornucopia of holistic healing modalities and unconventional choices you've made in your life, but I know it would be very helpful to our listeners to hear about what you call your "food journey."

Beverley: Of course, Erings, I would love to. In many ways, food is the biggest issue I have dealt with in an ongoing way throughout much of my life. (smiling) Other than money, that is. I often talk about how much I love food. That, for me, is an undisputed truth. In my teens and twenties, I was quite cavalier. After all, I grew up in the era of white bread and Cheese Whiz, of sugar and sweets.

Erings: Certainly sounds like the '50s I remember.

Beverley: I didn't have too much direction at home and had a very poor diet in my formative years. That actually would be putting it mildly. I especially adored meat, any kind of beef. My dad once joked, "You better marry a butcher, because no one else will be able to afford to feed your meat eating." I also loved fats: cream and cheese and sugars. I'd often put five teaspoons of sugar in a cup of tea and half of that cup would be cream. I know that sounds absolutely disgusting. At the time, it tasted incredible to me.

I do remember in the '70s reading the book *Sugar Blues* and beginning to see the light. Doctors rarely talked about nutrition back then. Even after I had my first surgery at age fourteen, I was told to go home and eat whatever I wanted. And believe me, I did. I really listened to the doctors on that one. And not in a healthy way.

Erings: Could you elaborate on that? I'm sure it would be helpful.

Beverley: I remember eating lots and lots of melba toast with butter. I would seriously eat thirty pieces of melba toast at a time—that is, three packages of ten pieces each. I never seemed satisfied. Of course, that is pure white flour and the butter is pure fat. I was doing what the doctor told me!

I know I abused my body when I was younger. In a way, this eating pattern followed me my whole life, perpetuating the inclination to the specific health pattern I developed: gluttony, sickness, and then what appeared like starvation. Even in my twenties, no one talked a lot about nutrition. Of course, I had heard the expression: "You are what you eat." It originated in 1826 by Jean Anthelme Brillat-Savarin and then was popularized via Victor Lindlahr in his 1942 book, *You Are What You Eat*, which then was reiterated by Adelle Davis in the '60s. So the idea has lived on.

Obviously, I didn't internalize the message. It certainly makes logical sense; but as intellectual as I was, I really didn't get it. How obvious and apparent that statement is. What you put in your mouth directly impacts everything about your physical well-being. Always has and always will.

Erings: So when did the real shift come for you?

Beverley: It came little by little. Even though we were juicing vegetables and fruits back in the '70s, we were also eating loads of unhealthy foods: packaged goods and large quantities of meat.

Erings: Careful. We don't want to upset corporate America.

Beverley: (laughs) It is undeniable, though, that a change is here. Awareness by individuals puts the demand on the companies to create healthier choices. So many people are writing about eating *real* food, not packaged food that is highly processed. As I trust we all know, the real food is on the outside perimeter of the supermarkets.

As far as meat, I mostly eat only organic, pastured beef, ethically raised. And where I used to eat 12- to 16-ounce portions, I now eat a mere 4-ounce portion.

Erings: I do see where the gluttony aspect comes in.

Beverley: (laughing) Yes, I really could pack in a lot of food at one time. I believe I'm resolving my karma from a few previous lifetimes on that one! I don't know what they are for sure, but this issue of gluttony and starvation seems to keep coming up for me—both extremes.

I have realized I do live my life generally in those extremes as part of an ongoing search for balance. Finding balance is a moment-by-moment elusive concept for me. Just when I think I've found it, it slips away again.

Erings: How do you eat now?

Beverley: I am extremely aware, conscious and careful. When I was very sick, eating in restaurants was difficult. Actually eating at all was difficult, because food usually would lead to pain, another reminder I'm in a body. I would say that I do eat 95 percent organic foods. I know some people think it is beyond their means, but you can buy large quantities of organic grains, beans, seeds and fresh vegetables, and eat impeccably healthy.

Erings: But you are not a vegetarian.

Beverley: Not even close! I still have a lot of food sensitivities. I stay away from gluten, sugar and corn. Corn is one of the most widely used and subsidized crops; it becomes everything from animal feed to sweeteners (like high-fructose corn syrup), so I have developed a sensitivity to it. Corn isn't even corn anymore because it has become a genetically modified crop. I buy local organic produce if I can. I do not eat genetically modified foods. I never use a microwave either.

Erings: You never use a microwave!

Beverley: I never have. My intuition when they came out was *stay away.* I haven't done the research myself, but I understand microwave radiation changes the molecular structure of food, making it non-food and unrecognizable to the body.

I also do not eat any leftovers because I believe the nutritional value of the food is lost. I also soak all my grains and nuts first before cooking them. Oatmeal gets soaked overnight because it helps break down the starches and makes it more assimilable. I soak and low-temperature roast nuts and seeds, too.

Erings: This all sounds *very* time consuming.

Beverley: Actually, if you are somewhat organized, it isn't really. In fact, I do not like preparing food at all. Of course, I love the finished product: the meal. The end goal. For me, anything that takes longer than half an hour, to prep *and* cook, feels laborious to me.

Erings: So how do you generally prepare your food now?

Beverley: A lot on the stove top. I do sauté veggies and chicken then put it over greens. For breakfast, I eat oatmeal with fruit. Simple, please, is my rule. I do think the quality of the food you start your day with is the most important factor.

From where I started to where I am now is like traveling to a diametrically opposed world. I can't even imagine the person who used to eat like I did. In a way, I know now that had I changed my diet back then, in my teens or twenties, my life would have been quite different. My digestive system was always being challenged, and it was already the weakest part of my system.

Erings: But you can't change that. Part of your journey.

Beverley: Absolutely. No regrets. Learn from the past, but don't remain stuck there. I know that dietary changes can radically improve health and well-being, and that is also a message I feel is important to share with as many people as possible. People will only change when they are ready, however. So I try to lead by example and by what I've learned as I've walked, or sometimes crawled, this journey to health.

Erings: Do you ask yourself if you can stay healthy this time?

Beverley: I believe one always has more to do, to keep growing and improving their health. Every day, I learn or hear something new that resonates with me. I try to incorporate that into my consciousness and to observe where my resistances might be. The mind, or our lower ego, is very powerful. I can talk myself into or out of a lot of things. I am very convincing, even to myself.

So now, I always attempt to come from a place of intuition. "How does that information resonate?" I ask myself. When I am sure about something, I am really sure. I believe part of this journey of health is for me to let other people hear that there are *always* possibilities.

Again, it's about taking personal responsibility, instead of living in a place of fear or complacency. We hear all the time now about connecting to your heart, where love and your highest good live. As I learned the hard way, it starts with having respect for your body, the temple we reside in.

It does sound simple, but when you do connect, it can make life easier and less stressful, even in the toughest of times. It's about trusting the inner rather than the outer. If only I had known that back then. Sometimes people are looking for quick satiation, especially when it comes to food, without considering the outcome of the choice they make. Some people can get away with it for a while, but once your body starts giving warning signs, I always wonder why we don't listen. Why do we wait until we are in a crisis to make a change? Interesting part of human nature. For sure that was true of me. But as you said, this was part of my journey. A lifetime journey at that.

Erings: You really have no regrets?

Beverley: Not in that sense. I think we all go to that place of "what if" or "if only." It is human nature, but the reality is: You can only go forward from this moment, this now, and use what you've brought from the past to enrich the present and the future.

Erings: On that note, all I can add is, "Well said!" We'll be back to continue our conversation…about money.

A Bit About a Lot of Things – Money, Music, Family and More Food

Erings: Okay, so we brought up the big one—money—before we went to break.

Beverley: Yes. I wasn't really going to talk about it, but money is probably one of my biggest issues in this lifetime. I think I might love money, even more than I love food. Hmm. Or at least as much. It is so big that I might not even understand the entire scope of it. Ask people who know me, and there will generally be a Beverley-and-money story.

I would say that the way I love money is not in the way people typically think about money and what it stands for. People say money represents success or power, or in spiritual terms, a way to spread energy. It is all those things to different people at different times. But I physically LOVE money. The feel of it. The weight of it. The look of it. I even have a very old money collection.

Erings: So what does an old money collection look like?

Beverley: (smiles) It looks like old bills that are no longer available. All colors, because in Canada we had pretty, colored bills before our toony and loony coins came out. I collect old money. I have lots and lots of very old coins, too.

Along with collecting it, money is a very big trigger for me. Pretty much everything in my life has had some money connection. I recently met with a longtime friend who reminded me of all the times we travelled together and how I was not willing to share the total costs, so she devised a plan where we would each put money into a kitty for shared expenses, like taxis and tips, etc. As far as paying, we would get our own bills so she didn't feel like she was not paying her share.

Then there's a kind of cute money story, from another old friend of mine. We had not seen each other in years and reconnected unexpectedly. She told me that her very first memory of meeting me was when she was six and I was five. When she walked into my bedroom, I looked up momentarily as I was thoroughly engrossed in counting the pennies spread all over my bed.

I interestingly don't remember that at all, but I can bet it is very accurate. I still love counting money. It has become a very sore spot for some people who know me well, like my ex and my daughter. They know not to mess with me about money. Heaven forbid that someone should owe me money, or forget to pay me if I've put out money for them. Like an elephant, my animal totem, I never forget. I often say it's a matter of principle. I'll lend you the money, but you better pay me back! I used to get very worked up about that issue. Nowadays I understand that in many ways I carry that money energy for most of the people I attract into my life and seem to be the one who has somehow figured out how to support others with their own money issues by having transformed mine. Hope that makes some sense.

Erings: Lots of people have money issues, but would you share how it is different for you?

Beverley: I confess that throughout much of my younger life I had an incredibly strong wish to be famous and rich. One had to go with the other. When I was in university, I did this timeline on what I hoped to achieve in the next twenty years. I remember that I had seriously intended to be independently wealthy by age thirty-five.

Erings: And?

Beverley: (laughs) Well, that definitely did not happen. I guess life got in the way and it seems my path was about something else. Health.

Erings: Well, you never know for sure. It could still happen. Would fortune without fame or vice versa have been as good?

Beverley: They seem to go hand in hand the way I envisioned them. Many achieve fame without money, and of course many have great wealth without fame. For me now, it's about making a difference, not about my attachment to fortune.

Having lived this life with health as a big part of my journey, I am hoping that through these personal experiences I might, in some small way, help others. When I was very ill, I chose to put aside my real, true dream and passion: to be a well-known songwriter. I sincerely believed that what I had to say could be told short and sweet in a three-to-four-minute pop song. It didn't quite happen that way—although there have been wonderful moments. I mean, I do have some great memories of feeling like we were almost there.

Erings: Will you talk about them?

Beverley: Of course. Back in the mid '70s, Doug and I, with a fellow musician, had written a song called "As Long As I've Got Your Love." Through a producer connection who liked the song, we got it covered by The Brecker Brothers, Randy and Michael, who were highly respected jazz players. Michael had played on the Blood, Sweat and Tears album with Al Kooper, "Child Is Father To The Man." Randy played trumpet and flugelhorn and Michael, who died in 2007, played trumpet.

The album, *Don't Stop the Music,* was recorded for Atlantic Records and released in 1977. The coolest part was that the producer flew Doug and me down to New York to sing backup on the track. So, here we are, feeling very important and extremely excited, flying to New York City to sing backup on The Brecker Brothers' version of our song.

When we got to Atlantic studios, we were the only musicians around, but we were told that Ringo had recorded in Studio A, where we now stood, the night before. And, The Rolling Stones had been in Studio B. It was like we were almost there. Rubbing shoulders, if only in spirit, with some of the greats of the music business.

On that New York trip, we also happened to run into the great "Pretty Purdie," Bernard Purdie, on the stairs outside his flat as we were leaving the studio. Purdie was, and still is, an influential R&B, soul and funk drummer. Doug had known him back in his days spent in New York as a doorman at the famous Night Owl Café, so it was a friendly and unexpected reunion for the two of them.

We felt that we were catching a successful vibe. Were we on the road to success? We recorded some of our songs with United Artists through a publishing friend at Warner Chappell Music, and we got some high-profile notoriety in Canada. We appeared on popular television shows both locally and out west.

Television appearance on Music Machine, 1975

Those were very optimistic and positive times. However, we still had not achieved the heights that I, at least, had envisioned. Not quite yet. The memories are great, though.

Erings: I can hear how it seemed you were getting close. Ringo and The Rolling Stones…that is quite an interesting energy to follow into the studio.

Beverley: Yes, we did feel we were really close. Another powerfully memorable time was in 1991. We had written a song called "A Different World," and when people heard it, they were visibly moved by the lyrics. Still happens today.

Back then, I submitted the song to a local songwriting competition and we won the first-place prize! It was a great affirmation. We got lots of press and even sang it on local television. For me, this has always been my definitive contribution. We recently did a current version of the song and I still have visions of the song being my "*it*" song. *"And the Grammy goes to…"*

Yes…that has been an ongoing dream for me for a very long time. Now, it would be wonderful to see it go to a charitable organization and used as a theme song—a foundation like Free The Children run by Mark and Craig Kielburger, or to some other group that works to fight homelessness and poverty issues especially relating to children.

Erings: Is that the song's overall message?

Beverley: Well, the song is about recognizing the plight of those who are homeless and how the constant state of war on our planet must change. Free the Children is one of the charities working to really make a difference and to change things for those in need. It aligns with my personal belief that peace is possible in our lifetimes and that we can create a world that works for everyone, not just for some. The message is: We *can* make "A Different World." The song can still bring tears to my eyes, because I really do believe it is possible to create a better world and I continue to hold that vision. Again, maybe it's the rose-colored glasses, but as I often say, "I have seen the future and it looks good to me."

Erings: I agree and believe that you are right on in holding that vision! And in relation to the song…it's never too late.

Beverley: Absolutely. If it is the right time and the right song, it will happen. My daughter used to tell me that you are never too old to win a Grammy, even if you are seventy. I laughed and said I hope I don't have to wait until then.

Of course, amazing things can happen at any age. Younger people tend to take things for granted. As you get older, the experiences are more appreciated and savored. Hopefully, age also brings gratitude. Some of my memories are still so strong that they do feel like yesterday, and I stop and wonder where the years have gone. You may have fewer moments, but they mean more.

Erings: Isn't that the truth? As the old saying goes, "Youth is wasted on the young!"

Beverley: Too bad, but it often is.

When I think about my mother, who is now ninety-seven, she still has so many intact memories from a very early age. She remembers experiences and people who are no longer alive, except in her memory. Her stories always remind me she is such a special person.

In fact, her entry into the world was also less than welcoming. As the story goes, when her mother got pregnant unexpectedly with her, already having two small daughters, she wanted to terminate the pregnancy. So, she just went and jumped off the roof of the building. It was 1915 and women didn't have many choices back then. Thank goodness for me she wasn't successful in her attempt.

Erings: Seriously, your grandmother jumped off the roof?

Beverley: That's the story, but no one knows if it is really true. If it was, my mother was very tenacious in her determination to be born. I guess she just went along for the ride. Others, like me, might have been scarred emotionally forever by hearing this; but it appears not to have affected my mother detrimentally at all.

Erings: In spite of everything you've already told us, it does seem that your mother is a strong and significant positive influence for you.

The Golden Family...Lil, Niel, Beverley & Lani at Lil's 95th, 2011

Beverley: Yes. My mother *is* strong and resilient. Both she and my father were born same day, same year, so they have their sun in Pisces and moon in Aquarius. That moon position, I've often believed, gave my mother a cool, detached emotional perspective. Yet my dad kept all his emotions bottled up inside, and holding on to emotions is what I think ultimately led to his early demise.

My father always appeared cool and collected and was the most charming and dapper man I had ever seen. He was my first experience of unconditional love, yet he rarely shared his feelings. My mom says that he did to her, but I don't think he truly did.

When my brother and I would do something that upset my mother, she would automatically yell at us, as her first reaction. Then she'd say to my dad, "Louis, will you say something to these kids?!" And my dad would smile his smirky smile, turn to us and quietly say, "Hello." Of course, we'd all laugh and it would break the tension. He was definitely *not* a disciplinarian.

My mother was a yeller, but still doesn't admit that she was. They were this couple, who from outside appearances were very mismatched; but in standing back now and observing, I see that they were very right for each other. I know the chances of marrying someone born the same day, same year are pretty rare—something like 1 in 4,578. And he used to joke that she was older than him because she was born in the morning and he was born in the afternoon. I don't have their birth times, so it is hard to prove.

Erings: That's kind of interesting that they were born the same day same year and yet were so different.

Beverley: It is curious to me. I mean, they did have lots of common loves, like the love of dancing. They were incredible dancers, so smooth and in sync, it actually mesmerized people who would stop to watch them as they glided across the dance floor. My mother once told me she had dreams of being a professional dancer, but back in those days, it was a hard dream to fulfill. She was an extremely accomplished athlete, as I've already mentioned, because back then everybody would gather at the park to socialize. It was long before the days of passive entertainment like television or other solitary diversions. Being social meant gathering with friends and sharing interests in the park.

My parents Lil and Lou gliding across the dance floor, 1966

Erings: I would say today's younger generation is definitely missing that physical and social activity of earlier generations.

Beverley: As I've already alluded to, I didn't take after my mom at all in that way.

My mother was also very popular. Her nickname was "Boots." I wondered where that name really came from, although she recently told me it had something to do with having large female upper body parts and a favorite cartoon character of the day.

She tells me that when friends would call and ask for Boots and her father would answer the phone, he would jokingly say, "No boots here, only shoes." She still gets a kick out of that story. It is really charming and shows the innocence of the time. My mother has always been a very social person. In fact, she still has a friend whom she has been friends with since she was sixteen or seventeen. Some seventy-eight-plus years. One friend! It is hard to imagine in our disposable world.

Erings: I know how that bond of longtime close friendship can feel. And your father?

Beverley: My father had an interesting, but dark childhood. He was the product of an arranged second marriage. His dad was older and they sent this younger bride from overseas. She was from Lithuania and already had a small daughter who was sent to South Africa with other family members, so I know we have long-lost relatives somewhere on the other side of the world.

I can only imagine what that must have been like for her, to be uprooted, have to leave her child and come to this far away country across the ocean. Although very unhappy, she obliged her family; she probably did not even have a choice. She came to Canada and was thrust into being a mother to two young children, a sister and brother, from her new husband's first marriage and then she gave birth to my father and his younger sister in this arranged marriage.

The story has been told that when my father was four years old, he and his mother were in a closed room where a fire burned in a wood stove. He saw her catch fire, although it is unknown how this happened, and he witnessed her burning to death right in front of him in the room. He couldn't get out, as he wasn't tall enough to reach the door handle, and no one heard him banging on the window or the door as he cried for help. Eventually people came, but it was too late.

Erings: I can't imagine how emotionally devastating that must have been!

Beverley: I've often wondered about that as well. My dad would never really talk about it. I heard the story from his older sister who believed that his mother, Miri, was so unhappy that she caught herself on fire on purpose.

Erings: Really? That's difficult to believe.

Beverley: Yes. I would want to believe it didn't happen that way as well, but that is the story that has been passed down.

Now, my grandfather, Noah, has four young children and no one to look after them. His brother Simon's family took them all in and my father grew up in a family of ten children, six cousins and the four of them, the large extended Golden family. Boy, I could write another book of the stories that came out of that clan!

My father never had a chance to finish his education, as he had to go to work full-time very early in his teens. Before that, he even went out with his father, who was a rag-and-bones man, selling to the community from his horse and cart. This marked his indoctrination into the world of the traveling salesman, which he remained pretty much his whole life. My father also had a keen sense of humor and was an impeccable storyteller with perfect timing.

Erings: Something like you!

Beverley: Thanks. I hope so. It might just run in the Golden family genes. And people absolutely loved my father. Everybody loved Louie. He had an irresistible charm, was charismatic and had a genuine elegance about him. He was a really gentle soul and my sense is he was easily bashed about by the big, tough world.

Back then people didn't talk so much about emotions and what they were feeling, but I always knew that he really, really loved my brother and me. A family man through and through, he struggled to make a living to support us. He never got above the "get in debt" survival mode though. So, I wonder how much I vowed to never struggle with money the way that he did. It really affected his health, I believe.

Erings: Sounds like his emotions led to health issues for him, too.

Beverley: That is what I believe. It was still the era when men felt like a failure if their wives had to go out and work, so my mother stayed at home and managed the household as so many women did back in the '50s. She played mahjong with the girls, which she still does today, and was a contented wife and mother. I could definitely not have taken that route. I don't know how my mother really felt about it. She never seems to feel she missed out, and she does not appear to have regrets.

My mother is basically a happy person who is thankful for what she has. I think somehow I am more like my father. More serious and interior. I definitely have a rich inner life. I love people, but I observe a lot and that's I think where the humor comes from.

My mother has always been very out there in the world, highly social. Part of lots of groups, joining in activities and being the coordinator. She is tough and dogmatic. You always know what Lilly is thinking and she is very vocal with her opinions, even when no one asks.

Erings: So where do you think your way with words came from?

Beverley: You know, Erings, I've thought about that often. My mother literally gets all choked up when she has to speak and often can't find the words to express what she wants to say, so definitely not from her.

The happy Golden family in 1966 at Niel's bar mitzvah

My dad was a great teller of stories and jokes, but he was a man of few words. But me, I must have come here to be a word magician. For as long as I can remember, people have told me how deeply I touch them with what I've written to them. Many have told me they keep the cards or letters I've sent them, which has always been so nice for me to hear. Maybe it's my gift to share.

Erings: It is a lovely offering! You believe that it is part of who you came here to be, it seems.

Beverley: Again, every astrology reading I've ever had indicates that I have the birth chart of a writer, a communicator. That always stands out for me. In many ways, my life is about exploring this voice. I believe we all do have some divine purpose.

As an Aquarian, I've always wanted to make an impact on the bigger picture. On the whole. I remember my brother asking me why impacting one person at a time wasn't enough. It just felt too small to me. If you're going to make a difference, hopefully it's going to include as many people as possible. That's what I've always hoped for. For me, it's *Change The World, Make a Big Difference.* I always wanted to create as big an impact as possible—in the way that you have, Erings. What you've done is on such a grand and spectacular scale. It is the kind of extraordinary impact I'd love to have on the planet.

Erings: Well, I'm a bit overwhelmed by that, but thank you. You also talk a lot about wanting to be unique, unusual or extraordinary.

Beverley: (smiling) I do, don't I? Well, the ideas of *normal*—whatever that means—and *ordinary* were so foreign to me. I remember the time I took Lani for a pediatrician appointment sometime in her first year. Because she had been born premature, she continued to be in the below-average percentile for height and weight.

At this particular appointment, the doctor proudly announced that she was in the fiftieth percentile, so she was average. I literally took a step back and almost cried out, AVERAGE?! Pretty much in disbelief. Average was really not a common vocabulary word for me. He didn't understand my reaction as I asked, "Average, is that good?" because he was, of course, overjoyed about that. For me, his pronouncement was a little like the proverbial "kiss of death."

Erings: From the way you've talked about Lani, she certainly doesn't sound average.

Beverley: Yes, my daughter has turned out to be anything but average. I really don't buy into all those scientific statistics that create markers or limits for anyone. I sometimes hope that I haven't done psychological damage to her, because some people are okay with average, ordinary and normal. Maybe I would have been better off if I could accept them. I have bigger dreams, so I have bigger words, I guess.

Erings: And your daughter isn't affected by this?

Beverley: Well, people have always told me that they felt a need to please me. I never understood that too well. Even my daughter, when she was younger, confessed that she felt she could never really please me. My ex-husband also would say, "You're never satisfied. There is no way to please you or make you happy." That's hard for me to take, because that is never my intention.

I may not understand people doing less than the most they can, but some people settle for less. They are happy with less. I've always wanted more. What's next; what's bigger and better; what else can I accomplish? Having self-inflicted perfectionism, I probably have more issues with myself than others have with me. People have told me I have this air of authority or a regal air about me, so I don't know if it comes from that, or I brought it from a previous life. (laughing)

Erings: Ever tried doing a past-life regression on that life? (winks)

Beverley: No, but I guess that would be interesting because I am curious to see where this tendency comes from. Someone once told me it is like it comes from some really ancient sacred time. I mean, I have this great love and empathy for the elephant, so I don't know geographically if it's Indian or African, or Egyptian. (smiling) No elephants in Egypt, though.

When I have been really, really thin, I often appeared like a Kenyan woman. Tall, erect, with a very bony upper body. That would be very interesting to explore. Maybe I could write another book, on all my past lives. (laughs)

Erings: Yes, please let me know if you do! Do you think this perfectionism has held you back in other ways in your life as well?

Beverley: I do. Absolutely. Other than the enormous toll it's taken on my body and my overall physical health, I wonder if I've missed opportunities along the way by limiting myself. When you have to be the best or you won't do it at all, I sometimes wonder who loses. This has been a tremendous issue for me physically, too. I am a highly visual person. I see a lot of things that other people don't see. Not much escapes my eye, so when I look at myself I am not always approving of what I see.

Erings: Don't you think most people are like that? Especially women?

Beverley: To a degree, yes I do. I personally have a warped sense of body image. Although whenever I open up and talk about it, I find I am not alone. Many, many women do. Too many, as we are finding out. Visually I prefer the tall, lanky, melancholic looking body. The taller and thinner, the better.

Erings: Any visual examples?

Beverley: Sure. Uma Thurman and Gwyneth Paltrow have that willowy, graceful slenderness to them. And of course Daryl Hall or James Taylor for my singing men. It's a look. (smiling) I joke that even Twiggy would want to go on a diet if she was trying to emulate my perfect body image.

When I am thin, I have that look. This struggle is definitely a female struggle. I see it clearly, the more exposed I am to women's issues. In Elizabeth Gilbert's book *Eat, Pray, Love,* she comments that when she has put on weight, she exists more than she did four months ago. My interpretation of that is: "I deserve to have weight in the world." When I read that, it was very powerful to me because I was so very thin and I couldn't gain any weight. The idea that I wanted to have more weight in the world grew strong. I kept praying that I would gain some weight. Whatever way that took shape.

Erings: That is such a beautiful way to put it.

Beverley: Also, have you ever seen the movie *Conversations With Other Women* with Helena Bonham Carter and Aaron Eckhart?

Erings: No, I don't believe so.

Beverley: In the movie, there is a conversation about gaining weight: "I have earned the right to fill up other space in the universe." This is a common thread between all men and women, I believe. I still think men carry weight with more ease than women do.

My current mantra is "*I am ready to stay at the ideal, healthy weight in the world.*" Life certainly is an ongoing journey! Always be open to change. I sincerely never thought that too much weight would ever be an issue for me again, after so many years of being thin.

Erings: Yes, I agree that being open to the possibility of change is good. That's the only time that any change can ultimately happen. For some people, it is much more difficult than for others. I appreciate that you are open enough to talk about it.

Up next: Beverley tells us *all* about the exes…so stay tuned. We'll be right back.

Outrageous Encounters and an Excess of Exes

Erings: So, Beverley, you've talked a little about a lot of people in your life. So far, you haven't said too much about your ex, Doug.

Beverley: I'm glad you asked. Doug and I are still good friends. I think the fact that we spent so much time together, especially when we first got together, may have put a strain on our relationship. Too much, too soon. We were literally joined at the hip from the moment we met…today we would say 24/7. We lived together, worked together and spent every minute of our spare time together. Yikes! What *was* I thinking?

I'd have to admit that it stifled us both. I put a lot of my other interests on hold. Once we got together, all our energies were put into "making it" in the music business. We had become our own version of Sonny & Cher. I was a cool, detached, dry-humored vamp; he was the bubbly kind of emotional counterpart. So, at that time, it worked on stage. But I don't think it was too good for the relationship.

Beverley & Doug, 1976 – Our homage to "Sonny & Cher"

Doug had a lot of pent-up anger. He was a hothead, extremely volatile and you could never predict when he would explode. I, on the other hand, kept it all inside. My cool exterior was a cover for my suppressed, unexpressed feelings. Although I am emotional, it doesn't come out quite so easily. Just eats away at me inside. We were not necessarily a good couple for communication purposes.

Doug was a hairy Jerry Garcia meets Santa Claus meets Kenny Rogers. Actually, there's a bit of a funny story relating to that one. On one of our trips to L.A., sometime in the seventies, we had decided to go to a downtown L.A. nightclub. We were standing in line with everyone else, not even sure if we would get in. Word was spreading through the line that Kenny Rogers was going to be at the club that night...and some people in the line started thinking that Doug was Kenny Rogers. Again, word was spreading throughout the line and finally someone asked him to sing, which of course he did. Doug was never shy to sing. This seemed to convince them even more. That was quite surprising to me. People were oohing and aahing, not really sure if it was him. He played along and somehow they believed him. It was kind of funny, but I felt a bit embarrassed and uncomfortable. I kept thinking, "Why would Kenny Rogers be standing in line, with everyone else?"

Erings: (smiling) Good question.

Beverley & Doug 1975 – Doug looking kind of like Kenny Rogers

Beverley: Well, of course, he wasn't. In fact, when we got inside the club, Kenny Rogers *was* there, sitting in the VIP section up on a balcony in a private section, looking down on everyone else. It was surreal because now all the people from the line were looking at Doug, who they thought was Kenny Rogers, and here was Kenny Rogers, being Kenny Rogers. I remember when Kenny Rogers saw Doug, even he took a second look! Maybe he had a moment of wondering who was who. Kind of a fun memory that makes me smile.

Erings: ('70s picture of Beverley and Doug appears on the screen) I see the resemblance, I do! No wonder Kenny looked confused. You also talk about how marrying Doug was like marrying your mother. What did you mean by that?

Beverley: Well, I had always wanted to marry my father, so it felt strange that I actually married someone like my mother. A lot of things about them are similar. (smiling) Be careful if you tell them that. They don't see it at all. But I do. It's the way they react to things, their temperaments. I have now learned that my being Aquarius and their being Pisces was definitely not the most compatible combination. They both smothered me with love. Aquarians don't like to be smothered, for sure.

So, in my early forties, someone who was exactly like my father walked into my life and in a way became the reason I woke up and ultimately decided to leave the marriage.

Erings: Really? One person could do that for you?

Beverley: Yes, I suppose if the time is right. He was young and actually more involved with my daughter's television life than with mine. Something about his beautiful and gentle soul reminded me of my father, and something in me changed forever.

It didn't happen until sometime into his working relationship with Lani and then one day, I was struck by a thunderbolt of recognition: There were other men out there who were different than my husband. I could never again turn back to the relationship we had.

He became an integral part of Lani's and my life for several years. In some ways, I know I had been waiting for him to show up. I had a lot of friends born under the sign of Libra. Every October 6th, I would think that I had forgotten someone's birthday, but I never knew whose. It wasn't someone who was in my life at that time. I had people on the 3rd, the 7th, the 8th, but no one on the 6th. I'm sure you can already guess that when I asked him his birthday, he was the one born on October 6th!

Of course I wondered, maybe a little too much, what that meant. This friendship between the three of us went on for a lot of years. It catalyzed the decision to end my marriage. It became very clear that there *was* something very different out there and that my volatile relationship with Doug didn't have to be the norm.

Erings: See, Beverley, it is amazing how one person can change someone else's life!

Beverley: Of course I know that now. To be honest, I don't think he even knows that he was that powerful a catalyst for me. Maybe on some level he did know, but it's not something we ever spoke about. At the time, *The Celestine Prophecy* was incredibly popular and I gave him a copy. He later thanked me, after reading it, for introducing him to the spiritual world. Maybe I helped him in some way change his world, too.

We were intertwined for about six years and then when I got really sick, I broke off ties with pretty well everyone, including him. I know he is now married and has a couple of kids, which is what he wanted so badly. I hope he is happy and is still playing drums and doing music and filling his soul with his passions.

Erings: You have pretty much alluded to the fact that you don't have the easiest time with relationships of the romantic kind? Willing to talk about that?

Beverley: (laughing self-consciously) Oh boy. Here goes. This is another exceptionally big topic for me. The one I have always been the most uncomfortable with. I really struggled when I was younger. The boys who liked me, I didn't like, and of course the guys I was most attracted to weren't in to me. I always went for the "cute ones," the "everybody wants them" kind of guys.

Erings: I suspect that a lot of us relate to that.

Beverley: I have pretty much always been very unsure of myself physically and I never found a comfort zone with my sexuality. Generally, North American culture still has a very Puritanical attitude towards sex and sexuality; so with my early history, it became even more difficult for me to accept that part of myself.

Erings: That is definitely true, but things are changing and I see more women coming to a place of acceptance in that area of their life. Was there something more than just that for you?

Beverley: (smiling) Well, I suppose it doesn't help that I have so much air in my chart and that I live in my head a lot of the time. That somehow took me out of my body.

And, if you all remember, I was the head dragging along the body. In public school, I was fat for a lot of years. When I see pictures now, I wonder what my mother was allowing me eat! What was she thinking? She still denies that my brother and I were fat. She didn't see it then, and she doesn't see it now (picture of eleven-year-old Beverley with her brother and father flashes up on the screen behind them). Now you can all see what I mean!

Beverley at 11 with father, Louis, and brother, Niel
(My mother still won't admit how "chubby" I was!)

I also had buckteeth, so some cruel classmate—a guy I'm sure—nicknamed me
Bucky Beaver. In reality, it was just a difficult phase and once my teeth straightened

out on their own I was then told that when I got older I would charm the pants off a snake with my smile. (smiling) It never would have even occurred to me to try to charm the pants off anyone!

The good part of these childhood experiences is that I became a crusader for the underdog. I always root for the underdog. That is partly a characteristic of who I came here to be and partly a result of the experiences that shaped that. Childhood as a fat kid is definitely *not* easy. I had lots of friends though, and we had a strong supportive group. I remember having some boyfriends, but was afraid of getting too close. I was definitely a prude. Yet all these early experiences have given me an endless wealth of things to write about.

In my first short-lived relationship at age seventeen, my boyfriend broke up with me because I wouldn't have sex with him. I was way too naïve to go there. I remember being devastated and crushed by that.

Erings: You've written about a couple of situations that could have been dangerous for you if they had gone the other way.

Beverley: Absolutely. The first one happened in Los Angeles, with a friend I traveled off and on with over the course of three years. She was much more playful, at least verbally, than I was; she was also a few years older and a bit more sophisticated in her sex-education background. I thought she knew what she was talking about. In many ways, she was just as inexperienced as I was.

Erings: Two neophytes maneuvering their early twenties together. How perfect!

Beverley: Yes, and doing it in L.A. makes it all the more interesting. We had no trouble meeting a bunch of different people, a lot of guys, by hanging out at the beach or going to hip, local places. We were staying in a guesthouse on my aunt's property—not very elaborate, just a bed and bathroom—and my aunt and uncle had loaned us their old car. It was a 1950-something Chevrolet and we could only get it going by starting it on the incline of a hill. Fun times!

Beverley in L.A. starting our loaner car on incline of a hill. Seriously.

Anyways, I had met one guy in particular, whom I was absolutely wild about. Same name as my father, Louis; really, really cute; drove an exotic red sports car and had a home high in the Hollywood Hills. One night he gave my friend and I the keys to hang out at his house and I remember when we got there, we had no idea how to turn on the lights. His view was incredible—we could see all of L.A. lit up below us. We waited for him with only the lights of the city below streaming through the floor to ceiling windows. I went out with him a few times and then he proposed that we spend a weekend together. I think Mexico was mentioned.

Erings: That's a bold move. *You* said yes to Mexico?

Beverley: I know. I was incredibly inexperienced and maybe a bit unworldly. My friend had given me lots of guidelines on how to avoid all the intimacies of sex, how to stay safe and just play around. However, me alone with him in his house was about to become a recipe for disaster. I could have been in real danger.

Erings: Before you even took off for Mexico?

Beverley: Well, we were in his bedroom and I'm really trying hard to remember everything my friend has told me. I have a feeling none of it is actually going to matter, even if I do remember it. Now he's telling me to go brush my teeth and I'm replying that I don't have a toothbrush with me. Not sure how I planned to make it through the weekend without a toothbrush; however, he tells me to go and use his, because we're going to share a lot more then just toothbrushes this weekend.

I definitely knew I was in serious trouble if I didn't come up with a quick comeback. I'm pretty sure my quick comeback was, "What do you mean?"

Things went downhill from there as he assured me this was not going to be just a necking session if that's what I had come here for. I don't remember what happened after that, except the vision of a speeding red sports car, with me in it, comes to mind. I somehow ended up back at guesthouse, safely. I think he dropped me on the front lawn, and I didn't see him or hear from him again.

Erings: Sounds like you were very lucky in this situation.

Beverley: Yes, that one turned out well. Of course, I was crushed not to see him again because I had convinced myself that I madly loved everything about him.

Erings: Next one didn't turn out so well if I remember correctly.

Beverley: The next time was on our dream trip to Costa del Sol in Spain! You're right, Erings...that did not end up so well. I'd met this gorgeous Spanish photographer, Ramon. (pronounces the name with a rolling "R", laughing) He *really* liked me and we tried to hang out a few times, mostly when other people were around.

Beverley in Spain, 1970. Photograph taken by the baby lion cub owner.

I kept frustrating him by leading him on, so I'm told. He continued to pursue me, confident he could win me over. And my guess is, the combo of his looks and his profession had always been a winning combination for him. Up until that point, he had always been lucky with the tourist girls.

One night I agreed to go to his apartment, primarily because I wanted to see the two baby lion cubs he shared the apartment with. When he asked me if I was sure I wanted to come to his apartment, I did say yes.

Now, I don't remember the idea of sex being included in the visit, but my friend tells me that absolutely 100 percent I had agreed to finally have sex with him. I was sure I wanted to go to the apartment, but I soon found out he meant something else entirely than I did. I was still so very innocent!

Off I go with him. I'm enamored with, and a bit scared of, these absolutely adorable baby lion cubs, which he now put out on the balcony of his apartment. I of course asked lots of questions about his intentions with them, including what would happen as they got older and got bigger. Small talk, small talk, small talk. That can only work for so long, when someone has other intentions. He didn't really understand English too well anyways, so he would have been very happy if I stopped talking altogether!

Erings: Are you *serious* about the lion cubs?

Beverley: Oh, yes. They were exquisitely beautiful, just like Ramon. So he shows me around his apartment and when we reach his bedroom, the entire tone of the tour changed. I think he threw me, playfully, on the bed. I tried to get up, but he didn't seem to understand the words "let me up."

Then, things got pretty intense and ugly. He started to tear off my clothes. I'm yelling for him to stop and realize he's gone deaf suddenly. Everything I'm screaming and all my actions are saying "no" and "stop," but he isn't stopping. I soon was left with only ripped bikini underwear on. I was panicked and had no idea how to get out of this one. He was obviously in some altered state of being, functioning from a place of sheer animal rage. I could make a joke here and say that maybe living with lions hadn't been such a good idea, but it seriously was terrifying in the moment.

Erings: Wow, that is definitely not a situation you want to find yourself in, ever. Sounds horrifying.

Beverley: It actually does get worse. Then, he started hitting me. My body and then my face. I screamed and kicked and screamed and kicked some more. It was several minutes of extreme terror on my part, and out-of-control rage on his.

Suddenly, thankfully, as quickly as he had started, he stopped. He had come to his senses and he began to cry when he realized what he had done. He was now sobbing uncontrollably. Some of my terror subsided and I finally inhaled again, knowing I wouldn't be raped, or even hurt much more seriously than I already was.

He ran and got me some ice to put on my face, as my left eye had now swollen to at least three times its normal size. He helped me put on my clothes, which I believe were still intact. He insisted on walking me back to the hotel.

Erings: You actually let him walk you back?

Beverley: I did, Erings. His remorse seemed incredibly genuine.

When we got to the hotel room, my friend who had been sleeping, woke up and was visibly horror-struck. I do know this sounds crazy—and I apologize to all the women who have not escaped sexual situations so unscathed—but I proceeded to invite him in as he kept apologizing, saying he was so sorry and so hungry.

I have this picture of him sitting on my bed without a shirt or shoes on. He kept apologizing and reminding me he was hungry, so we ordered me a bucket of ice and him a ham sandwich. He stayed and cried and ate, and I stood with a huge ice pack on my face. I must have been in shock and disbelief, because I'd somehow diminished the severity of what had just happened.

After the fateful encounter with the Spanish photographer

Erings: I can't believe that you survived that one. I don't understand why you didn't report him to the police?

Beverley: That is a perfectly viable question. My friend and I had contemplated doing that, but we were leaving the next day to go to Madrid. And because I really felt his remorse, I didn't know what to do. Maybe that's not the answer people want to hear, but that's what I did at that time.

Erings: I believe I understand, but times are definitely different now and it would seem imperative to report something like that to possibly protect others from similar behavior by him.

Beverley: I absolutely get that...now. It was a long time ago. When we investigated our options, we were actually told if we did report it, we would have to show up if there was a hearing or any other legal proceedings.

Erings: You definitely suffered some consequences.

Beverley: I did suffer an eye injury for a long time. I wore oversize sunglasses for weeks after that. The other members of our tour group were vocally outraged and also thought I should have done something, but the fact is, I didn't.

It is somewhat ironic, because there were only two things I knew how to say in Spanish—and they might have helped me if I needed some help. The first was *"dónde está la playa?"* or "where's the beach?," which I never really had to use because we were literally staying on the beach. The second was *"no esta noche, tal vez mañana."* This means "not tonight, maybe tomorrow." I used that one a lot with all the guys I met, but this time it actually did not pay off for me. I was always safer asking, "Where's the beach?"

Erings: Always a jokester, Beverley, aren't you?

Beverley: I really want to say that although the story is horrifying in so many ways and has a serious and tense tone to it, when I talk about it, I just need to lighten the mood. Otherwise it would be too hard to retell. Again, I apologize to all the women who are shocked, but it was 1969. Things were different then. It is absolutely not an excuse, but I don't know what else to say, except, I'm sorry.

Erings: You are forgiven, by me, anyways. We all have things from our past that we would have done differently had we been just a little bit wiser. At some point you *must* have gotten more connected to your body?

Beverley: I have often asked myself that as well. When I was a twenty-one-year-old marketing student at Ryerson hanging out with the Radio and Television Arts guys, I had a crush on one of the more intellectual guys in the course. We dated for a bit and I remember concocting this grand plan for us. Grand plans were definitely a specialty of mine. Always figuring everything out beforehand.

I had gotten tickets to see James Taylor's Troubadour Tour in 1970; this was the tour that introduced Carole King to the world as an artist. Previously, she had been primarily known as a pop songwriter. So I had the tickets—which for me are not the greatest seats, last row of the theatre—and I decided to invite him as my date. The plans were, if all goes well, we're going back to his place and I was ready to let it happen. Well, those were *my* plans; I'm not sure what his plans were.

The concert was indescribably brilliant. It was the first time Carole King had taken off her song-writer-only hat and become a singer-songwriter for the world to see. I kept apologizing that our seats weren't better, but he kept reassuring me they were fine. I will never forget that concert, actually. I'd say lots of people who saw that concert will never forget it. When James Taylor and Carole King reunited recently for the Troubadour Reunion tour, it was a sell-out in very large venues wherever they went.

Even him, a business-like RTA guy, loved the concert too. After the concert, we did end up back at his place. His roommate was asleep in his bedroom, so we were in the living room. There was me, him and the floor…and it happened. It was really short, both figuratively and literally, and certainly didn't make me think that this thing called sex was that exciting. I remember leaving his place thinking, perhaps idealistically, that if he looks out the window as I'm walking away, then it means something to him.

Ering: AND…

Beverley: Well, yes, in true romantic fashion as I looked back up at the window, he was standing there waving and smiling at me. That made me feel good in the moment, but I still never saw him again.

Erings: Not too much else to say about that one. And there were more experiences.

Beverley: Yes, there was one before that. One of my very first experiences was with the son of my singing teacher. He went on to become an enormously successful songwriter and if I said his name, you all would know who he is. He was very cute, somewhat moody. He went to school out of town, but we'd meet up whenever he came into Toronto for the weekends. I really liked him and we played around and stayed friends for a long time. I remember taking him to the Riverboat one night to see Jackson Browne, whom I already loved, and he really liked him. He was very impacted by the singer-songwriter that Jackson was.

After I met Doug, I matched them up in hopes they might song write together. They were both Pisces, but Doug was much too intense for him. He was more than capable of writing his own songs, being a bit of an insular man. I have only run into him once or twice since, but I have some really fond memories of those years. I really wanted to "make it" as a singer, so I had started taking voice lessons. I strongly remember the first lesson, looking out of the window onto the crowded midtown street and saying, "When I'm famous, I will remember this day."

Erings: (smiling) But you in fact do remember it. Which means you must be famous! (winks)

Beverley: (laughing) Yes, I do remember that moment. It is still crystal clear. It's interesting the memories that do stay with us.

Erings: You seem to have strong memories, lots of them, and remember them in vivid detail.

Beverley: I do. I feel really blessed by that. I've always had a strong capacity to remember. It really works in your favor when you are a student. It's not quite a photographic memory, yet it is a way I synthesize the world by assimilating information.

I see my mind as a huge filing cabinet or instantly accessible library in my brain. My mother has an immaculate memory, too. Always has. I think more than just having the memory, it is about retrieving the exact detail I need and then being able to apply my deductive capabilities as needed. When I write, my mind assimilates all this information and organizes most of it by the time it hits the page.

Erings: Ah, the blessing of being a writer! Well, Beverley, we certainly have covered a lot of ground and yet it feels like we haven't even scratched the surface. You have travelled a lot and some of the experiences are outright intriguing, to say the least.

Beverley: Yes, I have travelled quite a bit, even though at times I feel so homebound. Most recently, a lot of my travels have been with my daughter, both because of her television series and just for mother-daughter time, too.

I strongly remember two times we were in New York when monumental, world-shattering events happened. The first was on February 26, 1993, the first bombing of the World Trade Center, where its lower levels were damaged. In fact, the attack had been intended to knock the first tower into the second to bring them both down, but it had less of an impact then planned. We were in a television studio almost underground, just blocks away, so we felt the effect and the force of the bomb. The second was on May 19, 1994, the day that Jacqueline Onassis Kennedy died.

Erings: Really?

Beverley: Yes, and going back even further, in the '60s, I was with my family in Los Angeles when Marilyn Monroe died, August 5, 1962. My brother remembers us seeing the funeral procession from the window of the restaurant we were in.

I was also in Los Angeles in the summer of '69 with my friend on August 8th, when the city was rocked by the Manson family murders of Sharon Tate and the others who were at the house at the time. Somehow these four events have been etched into my memory and I doubt I will ever forget where I was when each of these events happened. I also clearly remember where I was the moment I heard the news that John Lennon had been shot; I was meeting with a longtime friend I hadn't seen in awhile in an uptown café in Toronto. This unbelievably shocking news of his death became the topic of much of our conversation.

Erings: You're right! I believe that I too can remember where I was when those five events happened. These events touched us all on some level. Perhaps they defined our lives and the times, even if in subtle ways.

Beverley: That is absolutely true for me, Erings. But on a more upbeat note, as I mentioned, I travelled a lot with that one particular girlfriend in my late teens and early twenties. We've already talked about the main events—the trip to L.A. and Spain—but so many other funny things happened to us too.

Erings: Do tell.

Beverley: Well, in Spain, we were staying at what was supposed to be a five-star hotel, right on the beautiful white sandy beach. However, in 1969 Spain, that did not necessarily mean what you might all imagine. Five-star in Spain in no way compared to five-star in North America.

The hotel was nice enough, but at the beginning of the stay we found that our room was infested with bed bugs. We were not going to be able to stomach sleeping under those conditions, so we marched down to the front desk to complain, of course thinking the hotel staff would react quickly and send in the cavalry to move us to a new room. We were shocked and confused when all they could offer us were brooms.

Erings: Brooms?

Beverley: (laughing) That's what we said, but believe me, we certainly weren't laughing at the time. We didn't understand what they wanted us to do. So we asked them to explain. No one understood English all too well.

Then they started hitting the air with the brooms, lifting the broom up and then slapping down into the air. At one point, when we still didn't get it, they starting hitting the sofa. Oh no. Were they kidding us? They wanted us to beat the bugs with the brooms. We were definitely too much like princesses to accept that as the only course of action, so we refused.

Erings: What were your options?

Beverley: Being exceedingly resourceful, we created our own brand-new option. We staged a sleep-in, right smack in the middle of the lobby of the hotel. We came down in our pajamas and robes, with our pillows in hand. Naturally, we had checked them first to ensure they were clear of bed bugs. We proceeded to lie down on the sofas in the hotel lobby. That certainly got their attention and although I don't 100 percent remember the outcome, I do know we felt victorious. We definitely did not sleep in the beds with bugs in our room. They either moved us to a new room or switched the beds in our room.

It seemed that by the time we left Costa del Sol, everyone knew who we were: the girls who had camped out in the lobby and the *turista* who left with a swollen black eye. On to Madrid. Interestingly, I can't remember anything about that trip beyond the bed bugs and the lions on the balcony. Maybe that was enough.

Erings: I can certainly understand why! That would have been enough for me. But you traveled more after that.

Beverley: Yes, another trip we really enjoyed was the trip to England. I mean the energy of London is, or was, quite wonderful in the late '60s, early '70s. Hyde Park and Carnaby Street. The London Zoo, the Tate Gallery. I loved it all!

I did get the chance to return to London in the '90s with my daughter for her television series and I truly think it is one of the world's interesting cities. I would be happy to go back to London over and over again. It is quaint and charming, but intensely diverse with so many choices to enjoy. I also remember that it is a very expensive place; in the early '90s I paid five dollars for a cup of tea. And they do not serve ice with any of their not-so-cold drinks.

Erings: London does have a certain wonderful properness about much of it.

Beverley: And it is a great place to connect with other favorite European destinations, too. On the first trip in the late '60s, we decided to take a day trip to Paris. Specifically to go to the Louvre, which I was so wanting to see. I had dreamed about the day I would get to visit the Louvre.

So we left London early in the morning and arrived in no time in Paris. The city was bustling with fast-paced energy, so we quickly succumbed to the hustle, taking in as much of the scenery as we can absorb in a day. We get to the Louvre, but there is no lineup. Seems strange.

There are very few people milling about in the grand entrance square, so we walk closer to the entrance, only to see a sign posted that says the entire Louvre would be closed for that one day only. I actually have a picture of the sign. CLOSED. What?! I am shocked, disappointed and actually in disbelief that we had chosen to show up in Paris the one day the Louvre was closed.

Erings: And?

Beverley: Well, that was it. We couldn't stay or come back, so our only choice for the rest of the day was to see Paris itself. We went to Montmartre and some of the other tourist sites. Paris is magical, but I still regret I never got to the Louvre.

I do have amazing pictures from both of those trips. Back then, I was doing my own black-and-white photography with my very old professional Pentax camera. All those pictures say so much of the time and the people. I'm very happy I have them. The characters I photographed in London are priceless. They speak volumes on their own.

Erings: There is something about London and Paris for sure. Too bad it is getting harder and harder to leisurely travel overseas.

Beverley: I agree. I would still love to go back to Paris, if only to finally go to the Louvre. Perhaps one day. Paris and Amsterdam. That would be a trip I'd want to take.

Erings: Any other trips you'd care to share?

Beverley: I'm already smiling as I think about this one, Erings. I guess among the most notorious trips I have taken were the times my friend and I went to L.A. and then on to Vegas.

And Vegas is quite another story altogether! We were—I would bet, this is about Vegas you know—some of the only people who went to Vegas looking forward to lying in the sun. It was July and probably one hundred twenty degrees, and we were at the pool with a mere handful of people, literally less then ten people including us. The nightlife in Vegas is all about the gambling and the shows. We never had any trouble meeting people and were quite surprised at how oddly these encounters always seemed to turn out.

Erings: I sense we are about to hear about some strange and unusual encounters.

Beverley: Well, it was now 1970. As you know, my friend had a highly extroverted and playful personality with men. But just playful. That was it.

One night, an older gentleman thought we were ladies of the night as we were walking by him through the hotel lobby. He struck up a conversation and started propositioning us. He was talking serious money for the time. I looked at my friend and with my eyes, I'm begging, "Please, let's get the hell out of here." That's when my friend kicks into playful mode and starts negotiating with him. I hear her now saying that one hundred dollars is not enough. I'm silently screaming, "What!" She is saying that one hundred bucks is not even enough for one of us.

They continue negotiating back and forth and she somehow gets him up to $200 for an hour with the two of us. Now, I'm scared. This is so out of character for me. I do not lead men on. At least I didn't think I did. This isn't fun for me at all. My friend is now laughing and she finally looks at him and me (I'm sure the terror in my eyes spoke very loudly) and says, something like, "No thanks, I think we can get more somewhere else. So, not tonight." I'm thinking of Spain and my one phrase, *"no esta noche, tal vez manana."* But in reality, not even tomorrow would be a consideration. This was definitely a never situation for me.

We start to walk away and I am demanding an answer from her as to what she was thinking. I'm absolutely petrified that this guy may find us and retaliate. My friend is now laughing at me and is in no way worried. I don't enjoy these insincere kind of pranks. I'm breathing heavily and watching behind me, not sure who may be following us, hoping that for this moment we are safe!

Erings: You *were* safe, right?

Beverley: Yes, we were safe.

Erings: And then another chance encounter.

Beverley: Yes, quite a chance encounter. Las Vegas also brought us an introduction to a suave, dapper and considerably older gentleman. He was soft-spoken with dark, slicked-back hair, which might have been the style of the day. He was quite taken with us and offered to escort us to any show we'd like to go to, all expenses paid by him. The first night we chose to see Anthony Newley and his one-man show.

I wish I could remember the hotel he was playing at, but most of those hotels from the '60s and '70s have been torn down and rebuilt again. We found out this man was from Guam. Money seemed to be no issue for him. In fact, we at some point got the distinct impression that he might have actually OWNED Guam. I don't know if that is even possible, but the way he talked about taking me on *his* private plane to *his* country, it just smacked of the possibility. I mean, there were no signs of bodyguards or entourages, but hey, Guam is a small country. Maybe it was safe for him to wander Vegas on his own and gamble.

Again, I was terrified of his intentions. My friend thought he just grooved on the idea of having a lovely young babe on each arm. He was, in fact, a charming man and continued to wine and dine us and send us to any shows we wanted to go to see. We saw The Supremes one night. And my friend was so thrilled that he wanted to pay for our meals and shows, because she was short on cash and was down to wrapping lunch leftovers in napkins and saving them for dinner.

One night he had offered to send us to see Elvis at the International Hotel. This was August 1970 and Elvis was, I believe, returning to continue his string of performances there. Neither of us were really Elvis fans, so in typical logical decision-making mode, we chose to see Dionne Warwick and forgo the once-in-a-lifetime opportunity to see Elvis. People still kid us about that one to this day.

Erings: In retrospect, it's easy to see how much you missed out by not seeing Elvis.

Beverley: Yes, and not too long ago, I got a phone call from my ex telling me to turn on the Elvis retrospective on television. It was a six or eight-hour marathon, and he thought maybe I would see myself in the audience. I had to remind him that we chose NOT to go and see Elvis, but to go and see Dionne Warwick instead. "Ohhhh, too bad," he answered. But, I remind people, I *really* liked Dionne Warwick. Don't forget I had even sung one of her songs at my *Hair* audition. Do I regret not seeing Elvis? I've never been that kind of fanatic fan of his. As I mentioned earlier, my youth was spent listening to Sammy Davis, Jr. and Steve Lawrence and Edie Gormé, Joe Williams and Nancy Wilson. My generation loved Elvis, but I wasn't listening to his music. The closest I came to Elvis was Ricky Nelson, but he didn't move his hips—so maybe to me, he was safer!

I mean, my record collection consisted of all of those I just mentioned plus Broadway musicals like *Oklahoma, South Pacific* and *L'il Abner.* I loved musical theatre and still had regrets that the "little Ethel Merman" people saw in me at age thirteen always longed to be revealed. I could never find the courage or the guts to get up and sing, even though I carried my trusty pitch pipe with me everywhere I went, even to that *Hair* audition. I just never took the plunge, worried that if I didn't sing it perfectly, why bother.

Erings: Before you fly too far off topic, let me pull you back to Vegas, Beverley. What happened in Vegas isn't going to stay in Vegas right now.

Beverley: Okay, back to Las Vegas and to Guam, which is actually what we called him. I believe he kept wooing me and wanted to take me with him on his private plane to *his* country. I was either very paranoid or very cautious. He never seemed to be deterred by any rebuttal I offered. At one point, he even invited my friend to come along as well. I wasn't buying into going off with him.

Erings: So what happened to Guam?

Beverley: Guam the country is most likely still there. Guam, the man and our Las Vegas escort, not so sure. I do remember him calling me even after I went back to L.A., still trying to convince me to let him whisk me away on his private jet. I do think he came to visit me at my aunt's house and we may have gone for dinner. But Guam went home alone, on his very private plane, to what we have always believed, to this day, was *his* island.

Erings: There is one more Vegas story, if I'm not mistaken.

Beverley: (smiling) There is definitely one more. I'd venture to say there is always one more Vegas story, Erings.

The same friend and I were back in Vegas, this time during the Christmas holidays. We had met these two guys—of course, there are *always* two guys. We never knew their real names, but to us they were Bud and Cece. So their story goes that Bud owned a burglar alarm company and Cece was a burglar.

Erings: They actually told you that they were a burglar and an owner of a burglar alarm company?

Beverley: We really did not want to know any more details, but that's what they told us and their friends substantiated it. We of course couldn't absolutely prove it, but being naïve, we never doubted that this was the truth. We thought, who would make up those kind of credentials?

Cece was tall and lanky with sandy blonde hair, and Bud was a bit stockier with black, slicked-back hair. I have this picture of them leaning on the bar in our hotel, looking like two guys who might have been members of the infamous Rat Pack. We had been hanging out with them, very innocently, and then they asked us if we would like to join their group for New Year's Eve. When we said yes, plans were made to have dinner and bring in the New Year together.

Erings: Were you setting yourself up again, Beverley? New Year's Eve in Las Vegas. Hmm.

Beverley: The evening did take a strange and uncomfortable turn before it even really got started. We were asked to meet them at their suite and we would all go from there. We arrived and Bud welcomed us into the room. Drinks had already been poured. There were a few other guys there, but no Cece.

Suddenly the bathroom door flung open and out strutted Cece wrapped in only a towel around his waist. He was either not planning to dress for the occasion, or he was just running really late. I couldn't figure out which.

I'm already uncomfortable, because this being-in-a-bedroom-with-one-guy-with-no-clothes-on stuff makes me very nervous. Everyone else seems to be laughing at the situation, when suddenly Cece jumps on the bed and his towel conveniently falls off.

Now, I was really nervous and uncomfortable. He says in a cocky voice, "Bet you've never seen one like this before!" Now everyone is laughing and as I'm turning away in utter mortification, I'm thinking, "This is the *only* one I've ever seen." I just couldn't count the fact that, at four years old, I got to witness my baby brother's circumcision. I mean, that involved screaming and blood spurting everywhere and mazel tovs and it would just not qualify as having seen one like Cece's.

Erings: (laughing) Oh my, Beverley! You certainly do get yourself into unusual and uncomfortable situations.

Beverley: (smiling) Do I really? Of course, everyone still thought this was hysterically funny and I was definitely not joining the group on that one.

The evening turned out to be really tense for me. I had trouble looking Cece in the eye, or looking at him at all to be honest. I did know for sure that I was not going to be going back to his room ever again, no matter what the reason.

Erings: (smiling) You've got to love Las Vegas.

Beverley: I do, even though I haven't been there in a very long time. Last time we went was with cousins and my young daughter, maybe she was twelve at the time.

There is a very strict code in Las Vegas about minors in the casinos. Just walking through, if we stopped for even a split second, there would be a security guard in our faces saying in some deep authoritative voice, "Keep the minor moving. Just keep the minor moving."

No leeway on that one, so we continued to just keep walking. My cousin, who can be a very lucky gambler, made sure that we stayed clear of her in case we might jinx her winning streak. Our family is not generally very lucky in gambling, and having more respect for money than that, I don't gamble. Maybe in other ways I am a huge gambler, just not when it comes to the idea of losing money.

When Lani turned nineteen, we took her to our local casino so she wouldn't forever feel like "the minor" who had to keep moving. On that day I think I was up twenty dollars, so I stopped gambling and quit while I was ahead. In true Beverley fashion, I still have the $20 I won stashed away in a wallet somewhere. Too bad more people can't quit while they are ahead, in all aspects of their life.

Erings: Good thought. Just not human nature a lot of the time. (smiling) I'm good letting anything else that happened in Vegas stay in Vegas for now, Beverley. When we come back, we'll talk about your really early days and the time in your life you mentioned before, when your talent and potential were recognized and you were deemed a "little Ethel Merman."

Filling in the Blanks

Erings: Beverley, you talk about your enormous love of musical theatre and how you had the opportunity to participate at quite a young age.

Beverley: I believe I was fourteen when I first went to summer camp. I really wasn't too keen on camping, so it took me a long time to agree to become a camper. Bugs, tents and sports in general did not appeal to me. My parents had found a different kind of camp. It was, to put it bluntly, a camp for prima donnas.

When I heard that the campers slept in chalets with indoor washrooms, I knew it would be perfect for me! Although my parents could barely afford it, they sacrificed a lot for me to go. This camp had a strong arts and theatre component to it as well, so I had the option to bypass what most people go to camp for... the sports and roughing-it part. My brother, on the other hand, got to go to the regular type of camp. Athletic pursuits had never been in my comfort zone. I couldn't even open my eyes underwater, so I couldn't pass my Red Cross test. I was a total spaz on the water skis, so I did a lot of screaming and falling. Plenty of dramatics, but not too much waterskiing. Resistance makes things so much more difficult.

Erings: Very true of everything in life, Beverley.

Beverley: I was carrying around a lot of fears that held me back in any serious pursuits of becoming an outstanding athlete. Of course, I say this somewhat tongue-in-cheek. Maybe I should have said, *any* kind of athlete. Any ball game was sheer terror for me. With my eyes blinking furiously and my hands in front of my eyes, I was definitely not the player you wanted on your team. At least, not if you wanted to win games. I basically sucked at sports.

However, I was great in the arts-and-crafts arena. Music and theatre were my strong suits. When I auditioned for the camp production of *Fiddler on the Roof*, I got the lead part of Goldye. Simple for me. Here I was, a fifteen-year-old playing the iconic role of Goldye with a fourteen-year-old Tevye. It was a bit of a stretch but it actually, in some wildly crazy way, worked.

Everyone's parents had driven up from the city and the buzz and excitement in the theatre was so palpable you could feel it. You could almost taste the delight these parents were experiencing. It felt like the audience believed they were coming to see an exclusive professional production. I don't remember being nervous, but a lot of people were talking about me and my co-lead, young Tevye. We were *very* big news. The play went amazingly well and my parents, needless to say, were— as we say in Jewish—*kvelling*, which means delighted and proud. Almost to the point of tears. Of course, my mother said I was the best one in the play. Thank you, Mom.

Erings: (smiling) Isn't that what parents do?

Beverley: Of course. But the production even got a review in the newspaper with the writer giving kudos to the two leads for their strong believability. Someone commented on the strength and projection of my voice and compared me to a "little Ethel Merman." There were no microphones, but my voice projected to the very back of the theatre.

It's Kudos All 'round
As Parents Assess Play

By ANITA EPSTEIN

It's refreshing to watch amateurs try their hand in live theatre. .

It's exciting if the group performing is made up of children — and if they happen to be your children the excitement can lead to heart failure.

And so it was last night when the senior campers and counselors in training at Camp Rockwood in Muskoka put on their version of Fiddler On The Roof.

Parents came 100 miles to see their children put on a production that was far above the usual calibre of a camper's drama group. Director Al Gorden sailed his crew through a difficult play with professional polish.

LEADS GOOD

The leads, David Zweig and Bev Golden, were almost professional in their portrayal of the characters

Tevye and Golde, a middle-aged husband and wife.

But I'm not writing this to criticize the play, nor the directors, technicians and actors.

How could I? If your little Larry was in the play — the show was excellent.

PARENTS PROUD

And if their was an Oscar for expression all the mothers (and some of the fathers) would walk away with it leaving Liz and Sophia gawking in the wings.

The lights of the crowded rec-hall dimmed. A young girl, Marion Stark, skimmed the keys of the old piano. Gary Magder and Addy Gluck played the clarinet and violin.

Children and parents stretched forward in their seats.

CRITICS COMMENTS

"See the slightly plump girl, third from the left in the chorus. There in the back. That's my daughter,"

exclaimed one proud mother to another beside her.

"Isn't she terrific — Toronto's answer to Barbra Streisand and where do they put her? In the chorus!" she whispered to her husband.

Some smiled with pride as they watched their children. Others whose children weren't in the play poked them in the sides asking: "Why aren't you up there?"

During the intermission, one could hear:

A father shout to his friend, "Did you see my boy?"

A brother admit, "My sister isn't bad at all."

UNANIMOUS

And everyone agreed that the play was terrific.

And it was. In 10 hectic days the children memorized their lines, learned their songs, sewed their costumes and painted their scenery.

The audience couldn't have enjoyed any other performance as much. There was pride in seeing the young portraying the traditional life of their elders, and for that traditional Jewish European way of life.

Tears were in the eyes of the grandparents who had come to see their grandchildren. Perhaps they were remembering all too well how life was once in a small European village such as Anna Tevna.

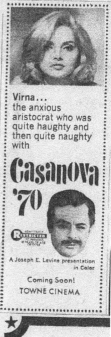

Virna...
the anxious aristocrat who was quite haughty and then quite naughty with

Casanova '70

A Joseph E. Levine presentation in Color

Coming Soon!
TOWNE CINEMA

RAY

Movie Starting Times

ALHAMBRA — Major Dundee 4.00 8.20 Genghis Khan 2.00 6.10 10.20 LCS 8.20
BEACH — Major Dundee 7.05 Genghis Khan 9.20 LCS 7.05
BIRCHCLIFF — Sons of Katie Elder 8.30 LCS 8.30
CAPITOL — Rotten To The Core 7.20 9.30 LCS 9.00
CENTURY — Glory Guys 6.30 9.35

ODEON CORONET — Help 1.00 3.10 5.20 7.30 9.40 LCS 9.05
ODEON DANFORTH — Help 2.00 7.25 9.30 LCS 9.00
ODEON DON MILLS — Help 2.00 7.10 9.55 LCS 9.25
ODEON ELANE — Help 2.00 7.25 9.30 LCS 9.00
ODEON FAIRLAWN — Those Mag. 1

My first "thumbs up" review, 1965

After that, there was talk that the owner of the camp would contact someone he knew, who knew someone who had Broadway connections. They sincerely thought I needed to be heard. I was excited and wondered if this night might be the start of my burgeoning showbiz career. At fifteen, I was very innocent. Not too much has changed actually.

Erings: But why not, if you believe that anything is possible?

Beverley: Indeed, everything seemed possible. I waited for news about some big audition or some introduction to someone important. Nothing ever materialized. I had also done the lead in *Brigadoon* the previous year, and then had a lead part my third year in the original camp production, so I was known at camp for my participation in all things theatre. This was the fun part of camp for me. I was less nervous about being on stage back then and I wish it hadn't changed for me. You never know what you might have missed. In some ways, that is why I am very happy that my multi-talented daughter has the guts to at least step in and go for it.

Erings: Sounds like you have some regrets?

Beverley: Well, not so much regrets, as wondering what might have been. I have questioned a lot of my choices in my life. I don't see them as mistakes. I believe we all have free will and that the karma we bring into this lifetime is still open for us to make choices from our free will.

I never wanted to have any regrets when I got older, but I still have the "what ifs." I mean, I have been sick more than I've been healthy in my life, so I wonder what I've missed in living this life path of ill health. I obviously can't go back, so I hope I can transmute a lot of the doubt and just see it as the path I agreed to walk in this lifetime.

Erings: The idea of free will is a grand concept for sure.

Beverley: Yes, it is. We all have a destiny, a karma, but along the way we have many opportunities to make choices that will shape an outcome. That is why I feel it is so difficult to be the one to have to make a choice for another living creature.

I'm very grateful I never had to make a life-or-death decision as a parent for my child. I guess I did, in retrospect, in the whole drama surrounding her birth. I sometimes wonder how parents who have to choose one path for their child, against others' advice, can bear the scrutiny. I also find myself questioning if that is their relationship karma at work. As you already know, I think it is difficult enough to make choices for ourselves—and I have always, or more often than not, gone against what might have been the popular choice.

Erings: Yes, but when you choose for yourself, you are 100 percent responsible for the consequences.

Beverley: Yes. Isn't that so much easier? In my twenties and thirties, as you'll remember, I was very cavalier about how I chose to eat. Here I was with serious digestive issues, already with two feet of my bowels removed and—here's a little something I didn't fully confess yet—I was addicted to Diet Pepsi.

Erings: Addicted to Diet Pepsi? That sounds very uncharacteristic of you.

Beverley: (smiling) Glad to hear you say that. It seems absolutely crazy to me now, but I would drink six to eight cans a day, or maybe even more. We would buy it by the caseload. I'd scour the weekly flyers to see where it was on sale. And there would always be a can opened somewhere in our apartment.

I remember my mother saying to me, "Don't you think that might be causing some of your health problems?" And sloughing off all responsibility, I'd say, "The doctors didn't say it was bad for me." The doctors generally didn't say *anything* was bad for you back then, as few ever talked about food and health as having any connection.

Erings: How times have changed!

Beverley: Indeed they have. As I mentioned earlier, I remember reading *Sugar Blues* way back in the '70s and hearing the mantra "You Are What You Eat," but I didn't really embrace and internalize it for a long time after that.

Paradoxically, Doug and I bought a juicer right after we first got married. A stainless steel Acme juicer, which I still have to this day, even thirty-five-plus years later. We were on the fringe of becoming healthy eaters. We actually lugged this juicer (which weighs *a lot*) to L.A. with us when we took our trips there. So, we were partially dedicated to changing our health; yet here I was, staunchly addicted to Diet Pepsi.

Erings: How did you get off that?

Beverley: In true Beverley style, I just decided one day to stop. Cold turkey. That's just my way of doing things. All or nothing. Ever the extremist. Nothing much in the middle. It was tough. I had symptoms of caffeine withdrawal for days, with jitters, shaking hands and mood swings, but I got through it.

Erings: Did you ever have any other addictions, like smoking?

Beverley: No. No. I am one of the biggest anti-smoking activists you'll find. When I quit Diet Pepsi, I was working for a major movie studio in the home video department and two of the guys smoked cigars in my office. This was way before anti-smoking laws came into effect. Nowadays, those two would have to huddle in doorways of buildings to smoke like that.

Even back then, I did speak up and let it be known that cigar smoke was exceedingly offensive. Of course they laughed at me, thinking it was funny. How the tides have turned! However, speaking up for what you believe in, and putting that energy out into the world, does resonate and can make a difference eventually. That's why I encourage people to speak up and be heard. I believe that is how change can happen.

It troubles me that so many people sit back in a state of complacency, complaining, but not doing anything about it. I think people need to speak up and fight for what they strongly believe in. Words are powerful. Changes can happen one person at a time. I've always found it strange when a person would say, "I'm only one person, I can't make a difference." It makes me want to scream. Of course, each person can make an enormous difference.

Erings: I also genuinely believe that each of us can make a tremendous difference by virtue of actively speaking up. So, Beverley, have you always been so outspoken?

Beverley: Not to the extent I am now. I've already mentioned how I strive for fairness at all costs. It was quite a rude awakening when I first realized fairness doesn't always happen. (smiling) But that's a whole other topic, right, Erings?

Erings: (smiling) Yes, Beverley, that's a whole other topic. Can we talk now about how you have moved around a lot from job to job? Is that something in your nature, or was it more about looking for where you fit in?

Beverley: A bit of both. I generally worked somewhere for a couple of years and then moved on. After my business degree, I did marketing research and then worked in a small film studio doing commercials and so on.

That's when a friend introduced me to an agent for singers. I went in and sang "Bye Bye, Blackbird" and within a week, I was paired up with a group needing a lead female singer. I had never been on the road, but our first gig was quite an eye-opener, as we ventured to a run-down, small-town hotel.

My bedroom had a hole punched in the wall beside the bed so you could literally see into the adjacent room. This was incredibly upsetting to me and I remember plugging it with a towel or toilet paper so whoever was next door couldn't see into my room. From that very first road experience, I knew I couldn't stay doing this, because again I was a little bit of a diva, and my environment was most important to me. Small-town hotels are generally pretty minimal, and saying that would be overly kind. They certainly do have character though. So I moved from group to group and even sang backup for some well-known, higher-profile performers, hoping to move up in the entertainment world.

Somehow, it wasn't what I envisioned "making it" in the music business would be. Then I met Doug and we decided to form our own group. That proved to be even more difficult. Finding and keeping musicians was so much work and intensely stressful. Rehearsing and trying to find personalities that would blend and meld. I mean, we had one musician—our guitar player—who was the core, but otherwise it was like the revolving door of musicians. We had a drummer who drank on stage. Nobody ever did that in the '70s!

Erings: That doesn't sound like fun.

Beverley: Definitely not. We also had a hypochondriac bass player who literally walked off the stage one night in the middle of a Steely Dan song, claiming that he had a blood-poisoning syndrome. Those were literally his words.

The song fell pretty flat without a bass player, but we kept on going as if nothing were wrong. Acting like everything was fine was an essential component to continue working in those days, too. And that, Erings, is only a couple of guys.

Erings: Any good guys?

Beverley: Well, we did have one mellow guy who did yoga standing on his head. He was the opposite of the guys who would go head to head with Doug's highly volatile temper. It was so difficult, but we continued to do it. We were on a mission to "make it" and at least back then, there were clubs and live venues to play. We worked in a variety of configurations, everything from a duo to a six-piece band. It was quite the life. Just *not* the life I had envisioned. So at some point, it wasn't very fulfilling anymore.

Erings: It sounds like the music thread runs pretty consistently through your life. Do you remember when it started for you?

Beverley: Well, yes. It began really early on. In public school, they offered school-based piano lessons and my parents signed me up. The teacher was a bit austere, definitely not a warm and fuzzy kind of person, so it was never much of a fun experience. We all got cardboard foldout keyboards to practice on at home. Can you imagine? I mean it was a bit crazy, but at least you didn't hear when you made a mistake! (laughing) Yes, it was rather a strange way to learn to play.

Erings: How would you actually become proficient with a cardboard keyboard?

Beverley: Therein lies the question, Erings. My parents eventually rented a piano for us and then I think we bought it. I did pass a few conservatory grades, but never got really good. That I must say I do regret! Had I learned to play the piano better, maybe I would have been able to be a self-contained songwriter.

When my brother and I were young, we'd recreate songs from our favorite Broadway plays. One was "I'm Past My Prime" from *L'il Abner.* I played Daisy Mae and he played L'il Abner. I remember we tried to dress up in makeshift costumes and I really wanted my parents to like it.

My mother's family is generally very musical. As I mentioned earlier, my mother was a rhythmic, sensuous dancer who had always dreamed of becoming a professional one. So there was always music playing in our house, though not necessarily the music the younger generation listened to. I do, however, remember rushing home from school to watch *American Bandstand.*

Erings: *American Bandstand.* Oh yes, I remember that, too!

Beverley: I can still see Fabian and Frankie Avalon, Annette Funicello and Connie Francis. I think they all were introduced on that show. And I loved the segment where they would rate a record.

American Bandstand brought popular music into the living room. That was a groundbreaker. No one in my group of friends ever wanted to miss a show. I believe the music permeated our lives as it came to us live in our living rooms daily.

Erings: Yes, it certainly was a big part of our formative years. Based on that picture, your whole family sounds musical.

Beverley: My brother is also very musical. In university—at one point we were there at the same time when I was doing my second degree—we both studied classical Indian music. I studied singing and he studied tabla. He has been a devoted tabla student, teacher and performer ever since. He plays guitar and sings, and has worked on several group projects. When we sing together, there is that incredible family blend that is so, so sweet.

Beverley and brother, Niel, graduating university, 1977

Erings: Did you have exposure to music in high school?

Beverley: Well, interesting story. In junior high, we all got assigned instruments based on how smart we were. Not exactly the way you would think someone should get to learn an instrument! In any case, I got stuck with an instrument I would never have chosen on my own: the violin.

Erings: The violin is so melodious and sweet sounding. Why do you say "stuck"?

Beverley: Mostly because I really wanted to play a horn or saxophone. I struggled with the violin and so did anyone who had to hear me play. It was pure screeching and perhaps more akin to torture than to music. I was never able to get close to being good at all, much less making music that sounded melodious and sweet.

It didn't help that the teacher was less than supportive. I'd say he had been teaching *way* too long. At one point he said he "hoped a bomb would fall on this class and blow it up." Hardly the words we needed to keep practicing. I guess we were pretty bad overall.

Erings: Really?

Beverley: Pretty close. He did get severely reprimanded for that one. Rumor had it there were some anti-Semitic undertones, considering most of us came from a Jewish background. I was too naïve to really believe that.

Erings: That sounds terrible, actually.

Beverley: It certainly left a lasting impression, as you can tell. High school was a totally different story. No music at all. And somehow dissecting frogs and taking Latin would never replace the joy that I felt from music. Honestly, our poor Latin teacher had her hands full with us. She was incapable of projecting her voice past the first row of the classroom, so generally it became a social period.

All of us, other than those in the first row, were having conversations amongst ourselves about everything but Latin. I often wondered why the teacher didn't get some kind of voice amplifier for herself—like a megaphone. That certainly would have changed the whole dynamic of the class!

I can't be sure anyone learned any Latin that year. Probably not. I for one, to this day, do not remember a single Latin word and feel quite confident I haven't missed too many opportunities because of it.

Erings: I would venture to say that missing Latin hasn't changed your everyday interactions at all. What was your favorite class then?

Beverley: One of my favorite subjects, believe it or not, was economics. Our teacher was a rather idiosyncratic, bespectacled gentleman who had, on more than one occasion, come to school wearing one brown shoe and one black shoe. I don't believe it was a conscious choice either. It just added to his quirkiness and gave us something else to speculate about in the cafeteria. I really got everything about economics—the law of supply and demand, markup and markdown. Maybe some people would have preferred Latin, but I loved economics.

Erings: Interesting choice, for such a creative person like yourself.

Beverley: Yes, maybe. Although I guess I was always creative, I also adored everything to do with business. Actually, sometime in grade 11 or 12, I knew I had to get out of high school. I was a superb student, but couldn't rationalize studying subjects that asked us to learn things I had no interest in. And seriously, those poor frogs.

My love of economics fueled my desire to leave high school in suburbia early, and attend Ryerson P.I. as a business student, majoring in marketing. This meant I could leave high school after grade 12 (it was supposed to be grade 13) and go directly into Ryerson in downtown Toronto. I didn't even have to pass go in this game, so it was perfect.

That's how I escaped the normal high school protocol and created a new paradigm for women business students. I was in a class of four hundred students, and maybe ten of us were girls. We ladies were certainly breaking new ground. And not to brag, but at the end of the program, I received the Ryerson Gold Medal as the outstanding business student. That experience as a business student was a profound turning point for me in my life.

Erings: But that turning point was not the only pivotal one happening in your life. I know this might be hard to talk about, especially so late in the interview, but are you willing to talk about the day your father died?

Beverley: This is so difficult for me. No matter how many times I've worked through this and spoken about it, it just doesn't seem to get any easier.

Erings: I realize how hard it must be, but after reading about how you dealt with it along with all the other challenging times in your life, I know it would be helpful for the audience to hear.

Beverley: Thank you, Erings. I hope that my stories might help others in some way, and that definitely goes for this one as well.

It was a mid-winter day and I was going downtown to school. To be exact, it was a Thursday, February 15th, the day after Valentine's Day. My father often drove me to school and then I'd meet him uptown later to pick up the car. He'd go to the steam bath, I'd drive home, and then I'd pick him up later in the evening.

The day seemed like the perfect clear winter day. The weather was unusually sunny for this time of year. I remember thinking on the drive downtown that he'd be proud of me and how pretty I looked in the new formal outfit I'd just bought for a cousin's upcoming wedding. That is what I remember, not too much else. I do know that day that it was just the two of us, although usually we would pick up a friend on the way there. But that day it was just he and I alone together, driving downtown.

As we approached the corner where he always dropped me off, I started feeling a bit apprehensive. I didn't want to leave him. I actually didn't want to get out of the car. To this day, it is a very vivid memory. Of course, he stopped and I did get out of the car. Before I closed the door, I leaned back in, looked at him and said, only half smiling, "Well, I guess I'll see you later." Almost with a question mark at the end of the sentence. I can't explain that moment in words. Something in me knew something I was not able to clearly identify or understand in that instant.

Erings: Something in you *knew*?

Beverley: Yes. Today I would refer to it as a strong inner premonition. Maybe a foreboding sense that something was going to happen.

We were going to be released from school early that day, and uncharacteristically for me, I decided with my best friend to take off even earlier and head uptown.

My dad usually got to the steam bath early anyways, so I thought I'd go up, pick up the car, and head home. I hung out for a bit with my friend, took public transit up to our usual meeting place, and saw that the car wasn't there yet. I decided to walk around the plaza and look around the department store to kill some time.

I came back a half an hour later. Still no car. This happened three or four times and in the meantime I tried calling my house to find out where my dad was. The line was continually busy. It was strange, as my mother generally played mahjong that day and should have been home by then.

But the line continued to be busy. At this time, there were no cell phones, pagers or any other mobile way to reach people. Only land lines. Those were what we talk about now as the good old days.

Erings: You said it, not me. Safer in many ways as well.

Beverley: So true, Erings. I finally decided to head back to stand at the department store entrance door that looked out onto the lot my father generally parked in. I kept looking out thinking, "He has got to be here soon." I saw the occasional car that I thought was ours and each time I ran out, it still wasn't my father.

It got later, darker and way, way past the time that my dad should have arrived. I kept using the pay phone to call home. The line was still busy. I phoned the operator to see if they would check if the phone was off the hook. At that point, I am officially starting to panic because I sense something is wrong.

The operator assures me the phone is not off the hook, but in use. I ask if I have an option. Can she interrupt the call. The operator replies, "No ma'am, we can only interrupt if it is an emergency. Is this an emergency?" Even though I don't know yet for sure, I feel like saying, "Yes, it is definitely an emergency!"

Erings: I can't even imagine your inner turmoil, Beverley.

Beverley: Now, another hour has gone by. I'm afraid to leave my viewing post in case I miss him. I am feeling angry by this point. Why is he so late? What is happening? Crazy thoughts run through my head. An accident? Tied up at work? My mind is racing. Of course, no one knows how to find me. I don't see any other viable options but to wait. By now, four hours have gone by.

I decide to leave my post and try the pay phone again. The line is ringing. I'm apprehensive, but elated. My aunt answers the phone and I say, "Hi, what is happening?" She answers, "Bevie (that's what all my family called me), where are you?" She had desperation in her voice. I immediately asked, "Where is my mother?" She says, "She's here. Where are you?" In that moment, feeling sheer terror in my heart, I ask, "Where's my father?" Without a moment of hesitation she says, "Oh, he's still downtown, somewhere."

Erings: You believed her?

Beverley: In that moment, I knew the truth. My father had died. He wasn't downtown or anywhere I'd ever see him again. My thoughts are interrupted by her saying, "We'll send someone to pick you up. Where are you?" With a tear-filled voice, I answer. I tell them I'm in the store at the corner where my dad and I usually meet."

"Okay, we'll send someone to pick you up."

Erings: And now you had to wait.

Beverley: And now I had to wait. I stood there for what seemed an eternity. Funny how we lose sense of time in times of ecstasy and agony. It was only thirty minutes, but it felt like forever. Crying uncontrollably, in shock, knowing the truth. Blaming myself, feeling hysterical, but trying to keep it together. But not keeping it together in any way, shape or form. I'm hugging the telephone booth for support. I'm feeling, well, I can't even explain what I might have been feeling. I was beyond feeling, in a surreal state. Is this happening to ME? The longest wait of my life, I believe. But so much more was to come.

Erings: Do you need a moment?

Beverley: Thank you, but I think I should keep on going so I can make it through this. I'm waiting and finally I see our car pull up—the one I've been waiting to see—and for a split instant, I think maybe this might have been some mistake on my part, a crazy misunderstanding. Maybe it's my father finally coming to pick me up!

But the only people coming to get me are my mother's sister and two men I didn't know. My aunt gets out, walks towards me and puts her arm around me to walk me to the car.

"Where's my father?" I cry.

"Bevie, it's okay, come get in the car," she replies.

"No, it's not okay." I cry again. "Where's my father?" Now I'm in the car. The two men are my father's friends from the menswear business. They are saying what sounds like crazy things to me. "Don't worry, at least he didn't suffer."

"How do you know if he suffered? He always suffered!" I blurted out.

"Bevie, calm down. It will be okay," one of them said.

"How can it be okay? My father is dead!" I'm sobbing. I'm screaming. I'm about to burst. How could this have happened? I just saw him this morning. He looked fine. We were talking. We were joking. We felt like father and daughter sharing love forever. Daddy! Daddy! How would I face never seeing him again? I'm inconsolable. He is the only person in this moment that I believe I've ever truly loved unconditionally.

Erings: Wow, your memory is so vibrant!

Beverley: In so many ways, this day is ingrained in my soul.

Erings: Yes, I hear that. So what happened next?

Beverley: We were driving and in what now seems like no time, we are at my house. Cars are parked everywhere. The house is overflowing with people. "Where's my mother?" I cry out. Another moment of panic. She's in the kitchen. She's here. She comes to me and hugs me and I'm hysterical. My brother is somewhere. My aunts, uncles, cousins and friends are everywhere. But where is my father?

"Bevie, he's not here," someone says. "Bevie, he died this afternoon."

"What HAPPENED??" I ask.

"He walked up a flight of stairs at the menswear office building, and he collapsed. He had a heart attack and died on the spot."

Erings: My goodness. Almost unbelievable.

Beverley: I agree. "That's it?! He's only fifty-one years old. He's never been really sick. Why couldn't anyone save him?" I howled like a wounded dog.

Apparently someone tried to give him CPR, but it was too late. Who's to blame? Me? Should I have stayed in the car this morning? All of us blamed ourselves in some way—my brother for having a fight with him, my mother for whatever reasons. What would life be like without my father? In those days, no one I knew had ever lost a parent at this early an age. I was nineteen; my dad was only fifty-one.

Erings: Things have certainly changed, I would say. Do you remember much after that?

Beverley: The next week was, without any doubt, the most emotional week I've ever experienced. The day of his funeral was torturous for me, with cold and blustery winter weather to match. But as his casket was about to be lowered into the ground, unbelievably the skies parted, the sun came out and it felt as if a very large presence was holding court over this scene.

I'd like to believe my father's spirit. I had been screaming and sobbing quite uncontrollably at the graveside. Anyone who was there would never forget "me" at the burial of my father. The shiva week passed in a blur. So many people coming and going. I was inconsolable most of the time. Friends came. Tears flowed and I was not sure how my life would go on.

Erings: But obviously it did.

Beverley: Yes. It did. It always does. Maybe things would have been easier if I hadn't left school early that day, because of course they tried to reach me at the school, but no one could find me because I had left early. I still don't know for sure.

Erings: What lesson did you take from this?

Beverley: I realized that we can't change the destiny of another human. I've come to understand that my father, in a way, sacrificed his life so that my brother, mother and I could have this particular life experience. But without getting too philosophical, it is what it is. What it was.

Most interesting of all, my mother seemed to be like a rock through all this. I'm sure she cried, but generally she stayed so strong. One week to the day of my father dying, practically the moment we were getting up from sitting shiva, her father— who had been overcome with the news of my father's death—died. It happened on February 22nd, one week to the day.

Erings: Really? That is almost unimaginable.

Beverley: It is, isn't it? And my mother went from mourning the death of her husband to mourning the death of her father—in one week.

Erings: That's one strong woman.

Beverley: And never has it appeared to affect her. Her resilience is almost unreal. In fact, resilient is a word people often use to describe her. One other irony is that when her mother died many years later, she died on the anniversary of my father's death, February 15th.

Erings: Wow, I don't know about everyone else, but I think even I need a break after that story. (turning to Beverley) Thank you so much for sharing that story. It almost feels like you relived it in the telling.

Beverley: I do every time, Erings. Thanks.

Erings: You certainly are brave, and it took tremendous courage to tell it in the deeply moving and powerful way you did.

Wrapping It All Up...
Not So Neatly

Erings: I'm still working on processing this intense story about your father's death, but I wonder if you'd mind telling us how you personally have dealt with it over the years, as I know it would be helpful for the viewers to hear.

Beverley: A long time went by before I was sure I had processed it, Erings. For years and years, the approach of February 15th would be very difficult for me. To this day, I still mourn the loss of my father and what it means to me. I've been lost and angry at times. I've tried to make sense of it. I continue to miss him deeply.

Erings: That sounds completely normal though, Beverley.

Beverley: Yes, I am sure it is. But, I've done a lot of work around healing his loss and allowing the love we shared to live in my heart. Maybe that sounds cliché, but personally I believe that love never ever dies. If we really understood that, perhaps it would be easier for people to move forward and not live so much in a place of grief and loss and anger. Once we truly experience the feelings, maybe we can let them go more easily.

I still miss him, of course meaning the physical him. I still see his smile and miss our connection. But somehow, it is still there. I dream about him. I have dreams where I am with him and I say to him things like: "Where have you been? I've been waiting for you to come home. I've missed you." When I wake up, those dreams feel very alive and real. I'm sure everyone who has lost someone they love has similar types of experiences.

Erings: Yes, I imagine that they do. It is probably a universal experience.

Beverley: Unfortunately for me, his death spiraled me back into a place of severe illness. Within six months of his death, I was sick again and my life consisted of periods of really bad health and then some moments of really good health. By now, you know that this has been my lifelong journey. When asked what my life is about, I think it is really "the journey to health." I've been sick and I've been healthy. I remember once, in my anthroposophy class, having a conversation about healing. The statement *"You can be healed and still have an illness"* left a lasting impact.

Erings: That sounds contradictory.

Beverley: Well, if you think about it, we're all here to have a physical experience; so in some ways, all of us have healing to do. We can heal at the soul level and still have another part of our being, like our physical body, have an illness.

You cannot only look at healing as being what occurs physically. We are souls who come to the earth plane to have a physical experience and we are all healing something we bring with us. When we experience a physical illness, it's a disconnect from, or something that needs to be healed on the soul level where it originated. So I get that of course we can heal on a much higher level than just our physical being. I also remember in Germany, the doctors telling me that the soul does not care if the body is healthy.

Erings: The *doctors* told you that? Wow! That is fascinating and perhaps a new way to look at life for many people. I personally, absolutely believe it and see how it does make perfect sense.

Beverley: Of course, we all want to hear about miraculous physical healing...but that can only happen if we heal, I believe, on a much higher level. To a lot of people, I appear to be a miracle. Many people tell me I have given them hope. Especially those who have seen me in my darkest moments where I was in so much physical pain that I could barely make it through each day.

These are people who have seen me and prayed for me because of how deathly sick I looked. But, appearances aren't everything. Because, with me, what you see is not necessarily what you get! I believe there is something much greater and grander than just this physical me.

I trust that I am being guided and watched over and everything is as it should be. There are people who fear physical death and those who welcome it. I want to be here in this physical body for as long as I can and hope to make as much of a positive impact as possible.

Erings: But isn't giving hope to even just one person huge?

Beverley: Yes, it is. Still, I would love to see it on a very large scale. I do realize that none of us can know the full impact of our actions or our presence from day-to-day. It's hard for sure to know, so that is where trust comes in.

Erings: Are you trying to control what you trust?

Beverley: Not at all. I guess it did sound like that. It's about practicing giving up control and remaining in a place of trust. (smiling) Practicing is the key word. I'm getting there. It definitely takes a commitment to do the spiritual healing work. I think the planetary shifts are happening quickly and people are becoming clearer and understanding that we all have a responsibility to be a part of that positive change.

In this context, illness isn't necessarily a negative. So many people have done such amazing healing work for themselves *because* of their illness. In fact, when you ask someone who seems to have the most debilitating health issue if they would trade it for something or someone else's, they generally would say, "I'll work with what I got, thanks." Their illness seems to transform something in them and from then on, I believe, they are on their personal spiritual path.

Erings: So true! Even people who were given even the worst disease or prognosis have told me they still would have kept what they were given.

Beverley: Yes. There are those who continue to live their lives through sheer will—like my mother. She just keeps saying, "I've got to keep going" and has in fact never faced serious health issues in her life. My mother has always been someone who never wants to say goodbye. It was a source of humor and frustration for my father, my brother and me, because she would always be the last one to leave wherever we were.

Erings: That's a curious observation. What does that look like?

Beverley: Well, for example, every week we'd all gather at my Bubbie's house—her mother, with all the cousins, aunts and uncles. And it always seemed that everyone had said their goodbyes and already left, except my mother.

We would wait in the car wondering, "Where *is* she? My God, Mom, come on already." But, she has always been the last one to say goodbye, so I hope she does keep on going. It would be my delight to have her around for a long, long time.

Erings: Sounds like you have already gotten your wish. Your mother is definitely someone to admire in that sense.

Beverley: Interesting that when I was really sick, I had fears that I would die before her. Of course, losing a child has to be one of the most dreaded things a parent can go through. I can't even imagine that. But I'm still here, and she is still here too. I hope she continues to be the last one to say goodbye for years to come. Right now, she is the last one standing of her family. All her five siblings, some of them younger, have passed on.

I never really got the chance to say goodbye to my father, so I'm working on healing all the longstanding issues with my mother, so that when we do say goodbye, all will be completed. Closure is essential and people who leave us suddenly don't really allow for that to happen.

Erings: Closure. Yes, so very, very important.

Beverley: I really believe—like you do, Erings—that we must follow some passion in our lives. I once heard that if you ask yourself, "What would I be doing right now, in this moment, if there was no chance for failure, there were no obstacles and money wasn't an issue?" Don't think about it. It's whatever comes to you as the first thought. For me, personally, that would be and always has been writing.

Erings: And, we are so glad you did. As one last question, what would you say—if you were to look objectively at yourself—has carried you through, has allowed you to survive?

Beverley: Hmm. Perseverance and persistence. Relentless, stubborn persistence—and for sure, commitment. If I believe in something, I am fully committed, all in, from start to finish. (laughs) And somewhere in all this I must be learning patience. So, the three p's: persistence, perseverance and patience.

Erings: Hmmm. Persistence, perseverance, patience—cemented by commitment. I like that a lot. Quite a powerful team.

Beverley, I really want to thank you. For someone who claims to be a private person, you are extremely generous with your colorful and rich memories and exceptionally candid storytelling. It's been a pleasure. I hope we get to do this again soon!

Beverley: Thank you so much, Erings. I have really enjoyed and appreciated this opportunity. And yes, I hope we will do it again, too! (smiling) Soon. To talk all about my next book, hopefully. Until then, I can only trust that all of us do the work we need to do so you and I can share some positive stories of hope.

I've already got a lot more stories to tell. As I always say, each of our lives is a constantly evolving work of art. A life in progress is a unique, one-of-a-kind piece of art. I like to leave people with three words at the end of every interesting or stimulating conversation…"To be continued."

Erings: Yes, I love that. To all of you out there, bye for now. If you missed any of our intriguing interview with Beverley Golden, you can catch all of our individual segments with her online at The Skye's The Limit website.

Until tomorrow, remember to be kind to yourself and to others. And, in the words of our incredibly open and remarkable friend, Beverley Golden...*to be continued!*